GOLF magazine's YOUR SHORT GAME

GOLF magazine's

FOREWORD BY

Instruction Editors: JIMMY DEMARET,

Illustrations by   LEALAND GUSTAVSON,

YOUR SHORT GAME

BOBBY JONES

GENE SARAZEN, LOUISE SUGGS

JOE FARRIS   *Harper & Brothers Publishers, New York*

GOLF MAGAZINE'S YOUR SHORT GAME

Library of Congress catalog card number: 62-9902

CONTENTS

GOLF magazine's YOUR SHORT GAME

Everyone who has played competitive golf, at one time or another, has had the shattering experience of a sudden loss of confidence in the midst of a round that had seemed to be going serenely enough. Almost always, this sudden deterioration can be traced to a let-down in the short game.

In a similar way, all of us have seen golfers, necessarily appraised as quite ordinary on the basis of their scoring, who could have elevated themselves to a much higher class just by learning to save strokes around the greens. Many times I have watched in consternation while one of my playing companions, after playing two reasonably good shots to the neighborhood of the green, would then require four or five more strokes to hole out.

In any kind of play, the lack of confidence in the short game is a deadly insidious thing which soon pervades the whole play from tee to green. A short putt is missed or a chip fails to get close, and the player becomes convinced that he must put every second shot up close to the hole in order to get a par. This places a burden upon his iron play, which soon breaks this down; and, in the end, his driving is affected as well. Immediately he sees his second shot missing the green or going into a bunker, he knows he has lost at least one stroke. It is possible to recover from a bad drive or an errant iron, but a missed putt is an irretrievable loss.

In point of fact, the short play should be the easiest part of the game. The stroke is simple and the main factors are nerve control and the ability to select the proper club and the proper shot to meet the varying situations. There is no part of golf in which the factors of judgment, experience, and just plain common sense can be so useful.

In this book are set out the precepts of some of the masters of the game. The effort has been to give the average player an insight into the problem of saving strokes and avoiding unnecessary losses. I shall not go so far as to say that any one precisely describes my own method. Nevertheless, the reader can be assured that these approaches, both mental and physical, have worked for some very fine players.

BOBBY JONES

PART I: PITCH SHOTS

In addition to being one of the finest professional caddies in the history of golf, Joe Horgan was also one of its most talkative. Caddying for two struggling amateurs one afternoon, Joe, as usual, rambled on and on about the exceptional shot-making ability of his golfing idol, Harry Vardon.

Tired of hearing how the great master would make even the most difficult shots look simple, one of the golfers, after executing a magnificent pitch shot out of deep rough, turned to Horgan and said: "Could your Vardon get out of the rough that good?"

Horgan never hesitated. "Get out?" he replied. "Hell, he was never in the rough."

1. FRED HAWKINS ON PITCH SHOTS

LONG PITCH

The ball should be played about two inches in back of the left heel. Although in this position the ball may appear to be opposite the center of the stance, actually this is an illusion due to the fact that the feet are close together, or should be. Shot is played mainly with hands and arms, little pivot.

RUN-UP SHOT

This is used when the lie is so bad as not to permit a normal pitch, usually with a two- or three-iron. Hit the shot as you would a normal pitch while remembering to close the face, cutting the ball from outside in, thus imparting a left-to-right spin that will enable the ball to climb over rough spots.

PITCH FROM THE ROUGH

Play this as you would a regular pitch from the fairway, except that you open the clubface at the address, since the rough has a tendency to close the clubface just before impact. Make certain that you hold your left hand firm throughout the swing. Apply a little more effort than for a normal pitch.

PITCH FROM SANDY LIE

Hit an inch behind ball and explode it with less effort than you would for a normal trap shot of the same distance. Make sure the clubface is not open quite so much at the address, since the sand will be firmer than in a trap, and hence will not dig in as much. A handy shot for Texas golfers.

POSITIONING THE WEDGE

By Bud Ward

San Mateo, California

Most golfers—even good golfers—have trouble with the wedge pitch for one reason. They don't know how to position themselves with the club. For one thing, the stance should be opened a full 45 degrees from the intended line of flight. The ball should be played midway between the feet. The grip should be "weakened," which is to say the left hand should be placed more to the left side of the shaft and the right hand more on top of the shaft to be kept in opposition to the left. About 60 per cent of your weight should be placed on the left foot. *But the most important thing you can do in order to position yourself properly is to sit down to the ball, just as though you were about to sit on a chair.* From this sitting position you can then take the club away low to the ground, as you should, and then accelerate the clubhead so that the ball can be hit firmly. Only by hitting the ball firmly can you create the backspin and thus the control that is the essence of the wedge pitch.

PERFECTING THE PITCH

By Sam Snead

White Sulphur Springs, West Virginia

Even among good amateurs you seldom find anybody who plays the pitch shot as it should be played. Most people have a tendency to pitch the ball as though they were half-heartedly hitting a full shot. They use far too much body action by over-pivoting and using their feet far more than is necessary. Then, at contact, they try to help the ball get into the air by scooping it. What happens is that the ball flies into the air with little or no backspin and then bounces all over the green. This type of golfer marvels at the pro who can throw a pitch into the green at a relatively low angle and then have the ball back up on the green. Properly played, the pitch reacts this way because the pro, in addition to restricting the action of the swing to his hands and arms, allows the flight of the ball to be dictated solely by the loft of the club. At impact, furthermore, he makes sure that the clubhead does not strike the turf first but the ball. *One way that I have found to make sure that I am meeting the ball first is to try to hit the shot in such a way that the clubface touches only the top three-quarters of the ball.* In this way, I am assured that the flange of my wedge or the sole of my niblick doesn't bounce off the turf before actually contacting the ball, thus nullifying any possibility for the loft of the clubhead to produce backspin.

GETTING PUNCH IN THE WEDGE

By Lew Worsham

Oakmont, Pennsylvania

Although the wedge has more loft than any other iron in the bag, few people seem to have complete faith in the amount of backspin this loft will supply. I have noticed many golfers—particularly when they are attempting a long pitch from, say, 40 to 100 yards away—who try to add to this loft by scooping the ball, finishing with all or most of their weight on the right leg. As a result, the ball takes flight in an exaggerated parabola and then plummets to the green, like a stone, with little or no backspin. *To correct scooping your wedge shots, you should address the ball with 60 per cent of your weight on your left leg.* Then, while executing the shot, keep your head as steady as possible. To do this comfortably, you will have to punch the ball. This is to say, you will have to restrict your pivot and generate almost all of your power from your arms and especially from your hands. After a little practice, punching the ball will prove to be not nearly so difficult as it sounds. After all, distance is never a factor with the wedge shot, since you can always revert to your niblick or even your eight-iron if the shot demands that you extend yourself with your wedge. And by never trying to extend yourself with the wedge, you will be able to finish your swing well balanced on your left leg, without so much as a suggestion of having scooped the ball.

20

PITCHING FROM TIGHT LIES

By Walter Hagen

Traverse City, Michigan

The worst mistake you can make in trying to get a ball out of a tight lie is to force the shot. By that I mean, trying to whip the clubhead through tough grass in such a way that the flow of your swing is broken. You are almost sure to "blade" the ball—that is, hit it clean without benefit of backspin—or, worse still, fluff the shot altogether, with the result that the ball remains at your feet. Since backspin out of a tight lie is next to impossible to obtain, you would be much better off not to rely on any backspin at all. Instead, you should strive to make the ball sit down by lofting it as quickly as possible, relying on the height of its trajectory to make it alight on the green. *I found that I could accomplish this without too much trouble simply by taking the club up very sharply on the backswing and then hitting the ball with the weight of the clubhead—almost as though I were dropping it—without striving for any follow-through.* This "dead weight" action pops the ball into the air.

THE PITCH-AND-RUN

By E. J. "Dutch" Harrison

Tucson, Arizona

On those links they got over there in Scotland and England, up there by the North Sea—do you know the wind blows up a gale, even in July and August? Now, a man can't play ordinary golf shots under those conditions, so some of those Britishers have invented a shot that I think is right smart, although most of the boys over here think it's stupid. I'm talking about the pitch-and-run. Like I say, you can't play ordinary golf shots when the wind is coming up a storm. You take a man sitting about 40-50 yards from the green, the wind right behind him. Chances are, he'll grab a wedge or a niblick, like he always does, and try to cut the ball in there, real cute-like. Know what happens? He knocks it straight up in the air. By the time it comes down again, it's bouncing all over the green, like a balloon in a cyclone. So now where is he? Why, in the bunker, of course. Now, if he had been a Britisher, he would have left his wedge in his bag, where it belongs. *He'd have pulled himself out a little old four-iron or maybe a three-iron, and then run it up there, the way he would a long chip.* Ain't no rule says you've got to use a wedge or a niblick just because you're that far from the green. Take your three-iron and run it up there. See if it ain't easier than you think.

PITCHING AND CHIPPING

By Gene Sarazen

Germantown, New York

Pitching and chipping are two departments of the game where you are either great at them or just so-so. When chipping or pitching, most tournament players use the same club all the time. In pitching, this would be either the sand-iron or the pitching wedge. In chipping, this would be either the nine-iron or the eight-iron. Pitching simply cannot be done with a nine-iron, particularly if you have to pitch over a bunker or some other such hazard. The loft of a sand-iron or a pitching wedge allows you to hit your pitches firmly and crisply so that the ball has plenty of bite. This sort of action just is not permissible with a nine-iron. You should devote more time to these shots than you do others because they are your sole means of making up for a mistake. Chips and pitches must be developed through practice; they simply cannot be bought off the shelf. *For both shots the club must be held firmly with the first three fingers of the right hand.* Do not open the face on the backswing. Rather, make the clubface cover the ball throughout the stroke. Let the loft of the club get the ball in the air for you; don't try to scoop the ball. And keep in mind that the shot is played strictly with the right hand.

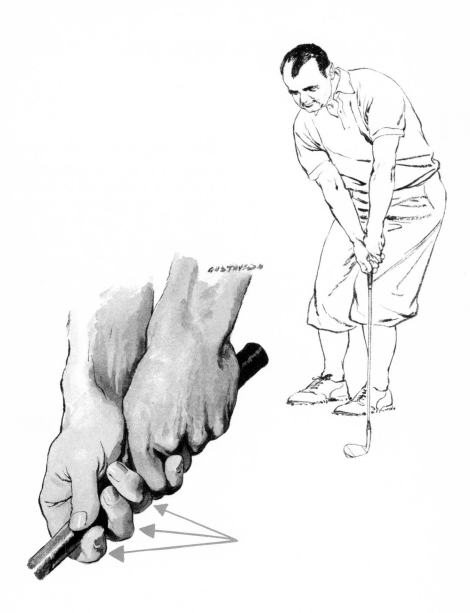

2. THE ART OF PLAYING OUT OF TROUBLE

By Lloyd Mangrum

with Robert Joseph Allen

Whatever else may be strong about his game, Sam Snead will forever be known first and foremost for his driving; he is, in the public mind, simply The Slammer. By the same token, Paul Runyan, perhaps the most accurate fairway-wood player in modern golf, will nevertheless forever be known best of all for his putting; it was as Little Poison that he made his headlines. And so it goes with Gene Sarazen and the sand wedge, Johnny Revolta and his chipping, Byron Nelson and his pin-splitting irons.

Getting out of trouble is not something that any golfer clever enough to become a national champion is likely to become famous for, at least not among the general public. But if you take a consensus of the pros themselves, the name that would come first to mind for this odd but not inconsiderable talent would be, by all rights, Lloyd Mangrum. A former National Open champion and one of the top money winners in golf since World War II, Mangrum is famous among his fellows for his ability to "work" the ball, as they say. Put him in a unique situation—in other words—and he will invent a way to get out of it.

A skeptical television commentator, who was unaware of Mangrum's ability to recover from seemingly impossible situations, was once describing a precarious chip with which Mangrum was faced to tie or lose a tournament in Chicago. "If he can only get the ball close enough to sink his putt," the commentator announced in hushed tones to his viewers, "he'll be able to tie for first place. Frankly, though, I think he'll be lucky if he can get down in three from that lie."

He had no sooner got the words out of his mouth than Mangrum proceeded to chip the ball into the cup.

Now pro at the storied Apple Valley Country Club in Apple Valley, California, Mangrum seemed the most logical person to interview on the subject of how best to get out of trouble: golf balls nestling in deep rough, stymied behind trees, lying underneath low branches, on upslopes, downslopes, buried in traps, and all the other things that can happen to a ball while playing 18 holes.

A phone call to Mangrum's pro shop at Apple Valley brought forth the information that he had just flown his Beachcraft Bonanza to the La Quinta Hotel in Indio, California. There I found him on the following day having lunch with Jimmy Demaret and Peter De Met, producer of the All-Star Golf television show. Bob Rosburg was slated that day to play Tommy Bolt on the La Quinta golf course, with the winner of that match scheduled to play Billy Casper the next day. On the day following, Mangrum was scheduled to play the winner of that match.

Mangrum suggested that he play 18 holes solo for me and deliberately aim his ball into troublesome situations, while I photographed his recoveries and recorded his explanations.

On the way to the first tee, he told me that he wanted to play the first two or three holes in regular fashion to loosen up a bit. He played two holes in this way while I tagged along with two cameras, several notebooks and a supply of freshly sharpened pencils. When we came to the 186-yard third hole, Lloyd selected a three-iron, teed up his ball, and took a smooth swing. The ball left the face of the club with that sweet click that tells a golfer so eloquently that he has hit a nice shot. It soared towards the green, landed directly in front of the flag, rolled up and up until it dropped into the cup for a hole-in-one!

After a short period of what might aptly be termed stupefaction on the part of both Lloyd and myself, we climbed into our electric cart and started for the next hole.

Had Lloyd made his hole-in-one the day when he was due to play whoever won the TV match of the day before, he would have collected the $10,000 that De Met has offered any player who makes a hole-in-one during the filming of his TV shows.

"Let's assume," said Lloyd later as he teed up his ball on the eighth hole, "that our man hit his ball off this tee into that group of trees over there on the right. Now, usually when the high handicap player gets into a situation like that he will more than likely try to get to the green in one shot, taking chances that even a touring pro wouldn't take. If it was a 200-

yard shot to the green, he probably would go in there with some kind of wood and take a chance on trying to drive the ball between the trees—a shot he could get away with maybe one out of 20 times. He would, of course, be much better off to take a middle-iron, say a four-iron, and hit the ball on a low trajectory out to the left, and a little short of the green, instead of trying to go through the trees and hope that he can then chip onto the green and one-putt for a par. If the situation is such in those trees, some underbrush for instance, for which a four-iron would have too flat a trajectory, then he should use a more lofted club, say an eight-iron, to play the ball back to the fairway through the largest opening in the trees, in whatever direction that opening might be. If he gambles and hits a tree, he'll probably wind up frustrated, with probably eight or nine strokes for the hole. Assuming that he *did* use his head and hit the ball with a safety shot up to about 50 yards short of the green, he would probably do a lot better with his next shot if he would stay away from the pitching wedge, which most of the professionals use but which I feel is for the experts. I think the higher-handicap players would do much better if they would stick to a nine-iron or eight-iron for the distance he now has to negotiate. Let's say he played smart and pitched with a nine-iron to the center of the green, so we'll give him two putts and a five for that hole.

"Now on this next hole," said Lloyd when he reached it, "we'll give him a good drive off the tee and then we'll give him a fairly good second shot ten or 12 feet from the green, leaving him about a 35- or 40-foot chip to the pin. Many high-handicap players in this situation will take a nine-iron or an eight-iron, or sometimes a wedge, and try to pitch it up. But I would say that if he would stick to a much more straight-faced club, say, a seven- or a six-iron, or possibly a five-iron, that he would, over a period of time, do much better. The important thing for the high-handicap player to re-member in such situations is not to loft the ball but to keep it low and keep it rolling."

"How about hitting some shots out of various kinds of rough and de-scribe them for me, while I photograph you doing it," I asked him.

"Okay," he said. "Over a period of a few months we touring pros have to play courses that collectively have every type of rough imaginable. Some have short roughs and some have a very long, heavy rough, and a type that you can only deal with in one way—hit down hard with a wedge.

"If ever you are in grass that is very long, very heavy, and very green,

Mangrum weighs up the rough before deciding which club to employ: wedge for heavy, five-iron for medium rough.

Playing to the green from medium rough, aim to land short and allow for roll. It is almost impossible to impart backspin on this shot.

Playing a wedge from medium rough, the club will tend to scythe through the grass rather than take a divot.

take nothing but the highest loft club that you have in your bag, and merely try to get back onto the fairway.

"Short rough is not too difficult to play out of. Often, it is feasible to hit a wood from such lies by playing the ball off the left foot.

"However, in playing a shot to the green out of medium to short rough, the player must remember that the ball can never be stopped very quickly. In other words, the fact that the ball is lying in the grass keeps the club from putting a great deal of backspin on it. Consequently, if you have a shot out of this type of rough, and you're where you might be able to reach the green, always try to figure to play the ball to land much shorter than you normally do, and let it take its roll up to the flag, because it's almost impossible to put backspin on shots out of short rough to medium rough. You can try all sorts of different things to impart spin but it will rarely help. Just anticipate the ball will run, and if you plan it that way, your shot usually will come out better.

"Long rough can produce a great deal of trouble, even to an expert, and I've learned from my own experience that sometimes it's better to take a penalty than to try to make what would be for the high-handicap player a miraculous shot, and wind up probably wasting one or two more shots. Though of course they *can* be made, still I say such shots are for the experts of many years experience."

"There are three types of lies," I said, "that are particularly difficult for the high-handicap player. One is the sidehill lie; the one where you're standing above the ball and have to drive it down towards the green; and the one where you're standing below the ball and have to drive it up towards the green. Please illustrate for me how you would play those three positions."

As we walked over to a fairway that had several tilts in it, Mangrum described some of the procedure these shots call for. "Taking the sidehill lie," he began, "where the ball is down below you, the one thing that you must be careful of, is staying well over the ball, because if you come up off it just a little bit on a sidehill like that you'll half top the ball, or worse, every time. Aim the ball to the left of your target and you will usually hit the green.

"Where the ball is above you on the sidehill, the first thing you must do is compensate by shortening your grip. If you don't do this, you will usually bury the club in the ground. You aim to the right of your target on this kind of lie. So there are only two things to think about: a shorter grip and an aim to the right to compensate for the fact that the ball will pull.

"The downhill lie, where you are aiming down and trying to get the ball off, is one of the most difficult of all. The difficulty in this lie is in getting the ball up. This can be accomplished by playing the ball off your left heel. The main thing to do on a downhill lie is to adjust your weight evenly to the contour of the ground. In other words, if you have a downhill lie, you must then lean to the left. Leaning to the left makes a downhill lie a level lie. And then make your swing as you normally would.

"In the uphill lie, which really isn't difficult because of the fact that the ball is easily gotten up on this particular lie, there's not much to compensate for, except that you again adjust your weight to the contour of the ground by leaning more to the right in order to make your lie more or less level.

"I would say that those are the main things to think about on these slanting positions. I do not wish to imply in any of the foregoing that these lies are not extremely difficult, even for the professional. It's very hard to maintain balance while swinging through them, and due care must be exercised."

32

There is only one way to deal with this type of rough—face towards the nearest fairway and hit down hard with a wedge.

"Another situation," I said, "that bothers a great many inexpert golfers is when they are playing to a green that is elevated and their ball fetches up at some point on the slope of the green."

"Those," he replied, "*are* very difficult shots. For instance, when a man overshoots an elevated green he's got a situation where he must get the ball up high to get back on the green—and the green slanting away from him at that, and at the same time doesn't have a great deal of green between him and the hole. In cases like that, the advisable thing to do is to try to more or less roll the ball up the bank and onto the green. Now, the only time that I would ever consider pitching the ball from the back of an elevated green is if there were a great deal of area between the fringe surface of the green and the flag. Such a shot is difficult but possible because of the fact that you have some room to land the ball on the green and let it take its natural run. However, for this shot you must have a very good lie, because if you don't it's almost impossible to get enough backspin on it to stop it before it rolls clear over the green.

"The same reasoning and procedure applies more or less in regard to the various other sides of an elevated green. The best thing to do unless you are an expert in regard to these lies and feel that the percentage is heavily in your favor when you gamble on a pitch shot, is to take a straight-faced club, a five- or six- or even a seven-iron, and more or less play the ball to bounce and roll up the bank and roll down onto the green, unless, of course, you have a trap between you and the edge of the green.

33

This is a situation where obviously you can't roll the ball, you must pitch it over the trap. Don't attempt anything fancy, just try to get the ball safely on the green, and then hope that you can make a long putt, or at least get it down in two putts, because if you try to play it too closely you might dump the ball into the trap, or hit it over the green, and wind up making a double bogey, or even a triple bogey."

"In connection with some of the shots we have just discussed," I asked him, "are there any hand positions that are important to the high-handicap player?"

"Well," he said, "I think a good rule to follow as far as hand position goes in connection with any iron-shot—even down through the woods to the driver—is for the high-handicap player and middle-handicap player —even the lower-handicap player, for that matter—to always keep their hands in front of the clubhead. Do not play any shot with your hands even with or back of the clubhead unless you are trying to play a very high shot over a tree or something like that, because keeping your hands ahead of the clubhead helps to eliminate hitting behind the ball, which is one of the prevalent errors in the playing of high-handicap players. If the hands are ahead your club has a good chance of hitting the ball first, producing a proper divot and causing the ball to fly correctly and pull up short when it lands."

"You are noted for your accuracy with iron shots," I told him. "How is the best way for the ordinary golfer to try and achieve 'dead to the pin' shots?"

"Well," said the master, "there are two objectives in iron shots: accuracy in distance and accuracy in direction. Hand control—a 'feel' for each club that can come only through constant practice—is the most important objective in the successful use of irons. I have always found," he said, "that the best way to practice irons is to start at the edge of the green and practice chipping. Then work gradually *away* from the green. As the distance increases between you and the green, you will have the occasion to become thoroughly acquainted with your hitting capacity with each club —a capacity, I might add, that will rapidly increase with this kind of practice."

He then gave me a demonstration of this type of practice. He began at a green, then went to a sandtrap, and then backed up to the various distances that matched the best use for every iron he had in his bag. He hit several balls with every iron—from bad lies and good lies, each one in a

34

different manner to illustrate the right and wrong way of doing it, explaining each shot in detail.

"From such teaching as you've done, and from observation while playing, what are some of the greatest faults you find in a high-handicap player, and which do you try to correct first?" I asked him.

"Well," he replied, "that's a very general question, but I'll do the best I can with it. When a high player, whom I've never seen before, comes to me for a lesson, the first thing I do is to discuss with him how long he has been playing, how much work he has done on his game, how many times a week he has been able to play, and how much time he can use for practice. Then, if I feel the man has a reasonable time to practice out what I teach him, I will watch him hit a few balls. It only takes about five or six swings for me to be able to tell him what his most drastic errors are. If he has about a half dozen errors in his swing, I explain what these multiple errors are and point out that the only way to eliminate them is one at a time, because no one can do six things at once. Of course, in connection with eliminating that many errors results are not gotten immediately. As a matter of fact, even after the elimination of two or three of his former errors the student isn't likely to notice much improvement, and he must be made to understand that before he can play well he must get rid of most, preferably all, of these errors.

"I would say that one of the biggest errors I find is a faulty grip. Now, I personally am very definite about bad grips and I make it a point to impress them with the importance of the grip, because I feel that that is one of the three most important things in the golf game."

"How do you hook and slice?"

"Trying to play a hook is very simple. All you do is turn the left hand to the right or clockwise to a straight position where all four knuckles and part of the palm become visible to the eye. The right hand is also turned clockwise, or to the right down underneath where the lines then formed by the thumb and forefinger, or parallel and pointing almost to the right hip. In the slice positions we reverse that, and turn the left hand counter-clockwise, where no knuckles are visible on the left hand, and the right hand is also turned counter-clockwise or to the left, where possibly two knuckles are visible."

"What about trap shots?"

"Actually," he said, "the trap shot is not too much of a problem, especially if you enter the trap with the right attitude. People generally use a

When you find your ball buried in a sand trap, Mangrum advocates playing the ball off the right foot and aiming about two inches back of the ball. The farther you hit behind the ball, the more effort you have to put into the shot. The clubhead never contacts the ball.
When ball is lying directly under lip of trap nearest green, the shot must be struck at least three inches back of ball and with power in order to hit it almost vertically up.

sand wedge rather violently and explode sand in all directions and usually nothing much else happens. The ball doesn't get out of the trap, or if it does, it's likely to go screaming over the top of the green into another trap, or even beyond it. Actually, trap shots that are played around the green can be played with a rather easy, soft effort; they do not have to have a lot of motion, a lot of swing, a lot of force. The only exception to this rule that I can think of offhand, is the one where my ball is lying directly under the lip of the trap nearest the green, and in order for me to get it on the green I must hit at least three inches back of it and with more force than is required in other trap shots in order to bounce it almost straight up in the air, but with just enough forward motion to make it land on the green. And speaking of hitting back of the ball in trap shots, it is very important to remember that you have to make sure that you hit the sand behind the ball at least one, two, or three inches, according to the situation, and visualize the club descending into the sand and scooping down and under the ball and through. The club never contacts the ball, because if the shot is done correctly, there is sand between the ball and clubhead at all times. The correct action is nothing but a simple scoop, that can be done very, very easily, without a great deal of effort. Most people push the panic button when they get in a trap. If you just take a little time when you get in a trap and try scooping the sand out from under the ball, the ball will come out just about every time, even when buried.

"The next important thing, in my opinion, is the backswing, because that's the beginning of the swing. There's a definite path that the individual must learn to take the clubhead back on. It is an action, in my opinion, that can only be taught by a competent professional, as should how to keep the head steady and shifting the hips. I always try to teach a very contained swing. I don't like to see long backswings. I like to see swings that appear to the naked eye to be three-quarter length, with the left arm straight throughout the course of the backswing and downswing. The position at the top of the backswing should give a feeling of firmness and tautness—not relaxation. If the various factors are right at the top of the backswing, it's very likely they will remain correct on through contact with the ball."

GOLF EXTRA: HOW TO WARM UP PROPERLY

By Joe Gerlak

The only reason anyone—except a professional—should ever play golf is to have fun and to relax. My experiences as a golf pro have taught me that when a player plays a good game—in relation to his average game—he is enjoying himself more, and relaxing more than if he is having a bad day. Therefore, it logically follows that to get a maximum amount of enjoyment out of golf, the player should come on the course ready to play his best game.

All other things being equal, I have discovered that the player who doesn't properly warm up beforehand is apt to have a bad day. The warm up is probably the most neglected aspect of most people's game.

The pros, the club champs, and the better golfers generally all know how to warm up properly, and are careful to do so. The typical weekend golfer—the fellow who could profit most by it—is generally the one who neglects the warm up. As a result, he tees off feeling tense and stiff, and cannot properly focus on the ball or properly swing at it.

The weekend golfer in particular needs a warm up. But he's just the person who doesn't seem to care. After having completed a busy week at the office, he rises early on golf day, drives to the course, dashes into the clubhouse and quickly changes into his golfing attire. Soon, he is walking briskly to the first tee. He waits impatiently while his playing partners or other early golfers hit their initial drives. Then, he walks on to the tee, unlimbers by swinging a club or two with each arm, and gives a mighty swipe at the ball, praying it will go down the fairway. Such a golfer plays under a self-imposed handicap. By not properly loosening up beforehand, he runs the danger of choking up early in the game; then spending the entire day trying to unwind himself.

I cannot emphasize too strongly the importance of a short practice ses-

Step 1: Wedge a club between your arms, bracing it against your back, and swing torso from left to right. This exercise helps loosen arm, back muscles, produce proper knee action.

Step 2: Take a couple of woods from your bag and swing them back and forth for a couple of minutes. It will take the kinks out of swing.

Step 3: Take a couple of practice swings with your highest numbered woods, then hit some practice balls. Work your way down to driver.

Step 4: Practice those putts. First start by making the short ones and gradually move back by one-foot intervals.

sion before a game. Athletes in all other sports warm up before they start actual competition. The baseball pitcher limbers up by throwing dozens of practice pitches. The runner will ready his leg muscles with scientifically planned short sprints around the track. The field-goal specialist in football sharpens his kicking during the pre-game practice session. They realize that the warm up helps loosen muscles, sharpens coordination and relaxes tense minds. Even the racehorse sprints and trots around the track before entering the starting gate.

Many typical golfers lament that only in golf is a player "cold" when he begins playing. This need not be true. The most experienced professionals arrive at the course well before a match in order to warm up.

Professional golfers each have individual styles of warming up. However they all concentrate on the same basic points. I recommend the following warm up to average golfers:

Arrive on the practice driving range about 45 minutes before the game. Don't bring friends or acquaintances along, because even their most well-meaning suggestions and comments are a distraction. Take the attitude that you are about to give yourself a brief private review lesson in basic golf techniques. As you proceed through the warm up, check yourself for a smooth swing; proper stance, balance, grip, and hand-and-arm action; straight drives, accurate putting, and sharp timing. It is important to remember that the warm up is only a conditioner. It is not the occasion to experiment with new ideas, or an opportunity to practice difficult shots, or a chance to try blasting your way out of a sand trap. Your chief concern is to perfect the basic shots. You can spend time on these more difficult problems in your practice sessions during the week.

Some courses have practice driving ranges, others do not. If your course doesn't have one, the best thing to do is stop off at one en route to the course.

Start warming up with the woods. To loosen your arm muscles and trim the waistline, pick two woods out of your bag and swing them easily at an imaginary ball for about two minutes. Then, put one back in your bag and begin hitting balls from the tee. I generally aim for certain areas out on the fairway. After the ball falls short, or over, or to the left or right of those areas, I adjust my subsequent drives accordingly. A good idea is to start driving with your highest numbered wood, and gradually work your way down to your driver. *But don't swing hard.*

After you have finished driving a few dozen balls, take out your irons.

Start with the highest numbered one and drive it easily from the tee. Then hit several balls from the grass with it. Repeat this procedure with the next highest numbered iron, then the next, and so on. And, again, *don't swing hard!*

When you have finished in this manner with all your woods and irons, take out your driver and slam into a few balls as hard as you normally do. Do the same things with each of your irons, starting from the highest numbered.

In putting, begin one foot away from the cup. It is very important to practice short putts, but, unfortunately, golfers don't seem to practice them often enough. Remember: *the most important putts are the short ones.* When you are sinking the one-footers regularly, try putting from two feet out; then three, four, five, and so on. Continue this procedure until you are scoring from about 20 feet away, and you are confident that you are putting accurately.

Follow your practice putts with brief exercises to strengthen arms. For example: 1) hold a club straight out in your left hand and raise it up and down several times. 2) Take several hard swings with two woods at the same time. 3) Place a wood behind your back and wrap your arms around the shaft. Twist your trunk from left to right—loosen up your waist, your knees, your arms and your back.

To conclude the practice, take the club which feels the most comfortable (maybe the five-iron, or four-wood) and hit a few lusty drives with it. This will give you an added feeling of confidence in your ability, and serve to brighten your mental outlook for the coming game.

Warming up may sound like a hard routine. Actually, it normally takes me about a half-hour to complete the entire practice. This enables me to relax for about 15 minutes prior to the match.

Lack of warm up is one reason why a golfer will find himself playing better on the back nine than on the opening nine. He actually spends the first nine holes warming up, although he is probably unaware of it. He loses valuable strokes and he runs the danger of compounding his first simple mistakes into larger errors as the game progresses.

Try warming up before your next game. You will have a better feel of the clubs, your muscles and joints will be loose, and you will have more poise in crucial situations. If you faithfully adhere to a preliminary warm up prior to each match, you will soon find yourself becoming a much better golfer.

PART II: TRAP SHOTS

Jerry Barber had been having a rough day with his approach shots, many of them wandering off line and catching traps. But each time, he recovered from the sandy beaches with the true touch of a master, leaving himself with short tap-ins. Finally, the inevitable happened. Jerry exploded a delicate shot that hopped onto the green, bounced once, then rolled unerringly into the cup.

As he approached the green, a voice from the gallery called out: "That sure was lucky, Jerry."

"That's right," Barber replied, "and the more I practice, the luckier I get."

3. BETTER TRAP PLAY

By Julius Boros, PGA

Mid Pines Club

Southern Pines, North Carolina

Let's take a logical look at the sand trap for a change. Although it is a "hazard" in the full sense of the word, it is not the monster that most golfers make it out to be. I can illustrate this by an example that should be quite familiar to most golfers.

I was playing in a pro-am tournament recently and I watched my partner hit a six-iron shot toward a green guarded by traps on both sides. He half-topped it and sent a low-flying shot to the right of the green. It splashed in the sand and stopped in the middle of the trap, about 20 feet from the pin. He slammed his club into the turf and then muttered a few words about his lousy luck. I couldn't help smiling because this man had obviously failed to see how fortunate he really was. If that trap had not been there to catch his stray shot, the ball probably would have hit about hole-high, taken several bounces and run an additional 75 feet before stopping in a clump of bushes about 100 feet beyond the green. As it was, he was only 20 feet from the pin with a good lie in a shallow trap. Why, then, was he irritated? Simply because he lacked the confidence to execute a good recovery shot from the sand.

You often hear someone say that "sand shots are the easiest in the game because you don't even have to hit the ball." In my opinion, sand shots are easy only after you gain full confidence in certain fundamentals of trap play. Once you learn these basics, traps will cease to be a mental, as well as a physical, hazard. You'll find yourself hitting approach shots more confidently toward tight greens—and landing in less traps.

If two conditions are satisfactorily met, there is no reason why you cannot play a wood shot out of sand. The two conditions, quite naturally, are a clean lie and a low lip to the trap.

Wood shot from sand: Playing this shot requires a good lie and a low lip to the trap.

Whenever I am faced with this type of shot, I weigh these two factors with great care, because should the ball catch the lip of the trap coming out, it would most likely cost me a stroke. When I have made my decision to use a wood, I take a slightly open stance and plant my feet firmly—but not deeply—in the sand. I play the ball opposite my left heel and even with my hands at address. Since I want distance with a minimum amount of body movement, the open stance cuts down on the amount of hip turn and helps to provide a more upright swing. Using no forward press, I bring the club back until it is almost parallel with the ground at the top of the swing. The turning of the hips shifts the weight to the left side as they lead the downswing, clearing the way for the hands and arms to come into the hitting area. I try to hit down slightly on the ball rather than scoop it. Hitting down prevents a topped shot. One way to get good results is to try to pinch the ball; that is, try to take just a pinch of sand behind the ball to guarantee a lofted shot.

With full iron-shots out of the sand, I make certain adjustments that differ from the wood-shot. For example, with a five-iron, I square my stance and play the ball midway between both feet. Here, too, my hands

45

Full iron shot: A compact swing and good hand action are essentials here.

are even with the ball and my feet are firmly set in the sand. With the square stance, the hips will rotate approximately 45 degrees and the shoulders 90 degrees. It is extremely important in this type of shot to keep a firm grip on the club at the top of the backswing. Any loose parts will only lead to a bad shot. As the downswing begins, I make a conscious effort once again to clear the hips so that the arms and hands are free to swing through the hitting area. The follow-through is important because it keeps the hands and the club going through the shot all the way. If the situation calls for a six-iron under fairway conditions, I take a five-iron, allowing for some counteraction from the sand surface and a somewhat shorter swing.

The most common sand shot is the explosion around the green. In this case, the distance to be covered generally varies from 10 to 100 feet. Any shot from a clean lie in this area always calls for one constant action on my part. I always try to hit approximately two to two-and-a-half inches behind the ball, adjusting the length and strength of my swing according to the distance to be covered. By keeping this same principle in mind for all explosion shots, it becomes easier to maintain consistency and, of course, accuracy.

When I prepare to hit an explosion shot, I plant my feet deeper in the sand than I do with the full shots from fairway traps. This is mainly because I want to get an idea of the texture of the sand. Since the rules prohibit touching the sand with the club or the hands, the feet are the only way to determine texture below the surface. Playing the ball an inch or two inside the left heel, I open my stance to restrict the usual amount of hip action. With an open clubface and the hands even with the ball at address, the clubhead will cut or slice the sand at impact and lift the ball out of the hazard. The most important factors in a successful explosion shot are to keep the hands moving toward a complete follow-through and to keep the head steady throughout the swing. Let the force of the right shoulder lift your head rather than just plain curiosity.

Two other explosion shots which are quite common also deserve some attention. From wet sand, I again try to hit behind the ball in the same spot. The only difference is that the sand must be hit a little harder and firmer since it will be more difficult to bring the club through the sand for a complete follow-through.

The explosion shot: With the feet planted firmly in the sand and the stance slightly open, the shot is always hit between two and two-and-a-half inches behind the ball with an open clubface and a complete follow-through.

With a buried lie, the clubface should be slightly closed since you want to take maximum advantage of the force of the clubhead. Closing the face assures a more pronounced explosion while opening the face provides more of a cutting action. The buried lie is the only type of explosion shot that requires more sand to be taken behind the ball. Sometimes, I am as much as four inches behind the ball so that the clubhead will be able to dig in and scoop the ball out of the depression it is in.

The one shot from sand that can cause a good amount of apprehension, even among the pros, is when the ball sets below the level of the feet. This is generally the case when the ball is in the sand and the feet are on the bank of the trap. This shot requires an exaggerated knee bend so that the hands can get in a good hitting position. Even weight balance is another essential as well as gripping the club at the end of the shaft. I try to use a short backswing with this shot because the more the movement of the body, the more I am apt to mishit the shot.

In preparing for any trap shot, I find it considerably helpful to take a practice swing in which I concentrate on hitting something specific, such as a blade of grass. This not only helps me get my swing in the groove, it also puts me in the proper frame of mind for the shot.

Low lie: Hitting a ball that lies below the level of the feet is a tough shot. It demands good balance and exaggerated knee flex.

PLAYING THE LONG SAND WEDGE

By Howie Johnson

Meadowlark, California

One of the hardest shots in golf to play, and one few golfers execute successfully, is the long trap shot to the green. This is a shot that must travel as much as 50 yards. It is a combination trap shot and cut shot, and should be executed with a full swing, the sand-iron striking the sand about two inches behind the ball. Most golfers have trouble with the long trap shot because they simply don't hit the ball far enough. *The key to making this shot successfully is to restrict the action of the left hand. The feeling you should get is that the left hand goes only as far as the ball and then quits, enabling the right hand to take over and dominate the rest of the swing. This "left hand quitting and the right taking over" produces a cutting action that enables the player to hit the ball 50 yards or more.* The long trap shot should be thrown right at the flag. It is not a pitch-and-run shot. Don't try to run the ball. Try to land it right in the hole. Don't worry—the ball will stop. After the left hand quits at the ball, it simply remains on the club in a passive capacity and is pulled through the ball by the dominant right hand. Most golfers, when confronted by a long trap shot to the green, do one of two things, generally. They either leave the ball far short or try to pick the ball out of the trap and invariably succeed only in hitting the shot thin, or "skulling" it right over the green and into more trouble.

MAKING THE TRAP SHOT LOOK EASY

By Byron Nelson

Roanoke, Texas

Most golfers have less confidence in making a shot out of a sand trap than with any other shot in the bag, yet this shot is an easy one for many good golfers, and the average player can make a dramatic improvement in this phase of his game by practicing these pointers: Settle your feet in the sand until you have a solid stance. Flex the knees until you are almost in a squatting position and be sure the stance is open. Keep the hands well forward of the clubhead as you address the ball and play the ball off the left heel. The face of the club should be open as this allows the sole to hit the sand first and prevents the club from digging into the sand. *Cock your wrists early and use a short backswing. Employ very little body movement, just enough to allow hands and arms to perform freely.* Pull through with the left side. Hit the sand approximately an inch behind the ball. Don't stop the action. Hit through easily and let the clubhead lift the shot. Don't try to kill the ball, since this natural impulse ruins many a trap shot.

HITTING THROUGH SAND

By Chick Harbert

Detroit, Michigan

Many average and poor players are at a loss when they get into traps. To begin with, the proper club, a sand-iron or sand-wedge, is needed. Since the ball is almost always lower than the objective, it is necessary to elevate the ball. To do this it is advisable to open the stance and the clubface. *Never strike at* the ball but always *through* the ball, *with an exaggerated finishing motion, so that the ball, if played from an open stance with the clubface open and with a firm swing, won't be left in the trap.* The player who hits at the ball will often bury his club in the sand and leave his ball in the trap. This is the worst thing you can do in making a trap shot, because it leaves you with your problem unsolved. It's better to go 40 yards past the green than to leave the ball in a trap. Most players could become more proficient trap players if they would practice trap shots. But in my time as a club professional, I rarely saw club members practicing trap shots. I know that in some cases players don't practice trap shots because of a lack of facilities but, more often, I think they fail to practice them because they are unwilling to accept the fact that they will get into traps.

SIMPLIFYING THE TRAP SHOT

By Bill Johnston

Provo, Utah

Many players use a different swing in playing trap shots than when hitting wedge pitches or other shots. In hitting sand-iron shots, they usually open their stance and cut across the ball in an outside-in fashion. This is generally recommended, but I have had much more success playing trap shots as I do my other shots; that is, hitting from the inside out, employing a stance that is very slightly open, and using a normal follow-through. When you cut across a shot, you invariably aim to the left and change the position of the ball at address. This has the effect of forcing you out of your normal routine, your usual way of hitting shots. *In a trap, I employ the same address position and swing that I would for a short pitch to the green.* The only difference is that I hit the sand first. Thus, for me, the trap shot presents no special problems and has actually become easier than some shots from around the green. Just prior to the 1960 French Open, I passed along this theory to a couple of young British professionals and they found it worked well. At my home club, I teach this system and the results have been gratifying. If you hit trap shots as you do other shots, you can't help but improve your game.

THE TRAP-SHOT SWING

By Bob Hamrich

Champaign, Illinois

In hitting trap shots from within 20 yards of the pin, I explode the ball by using the same swing I would in hitting a fairway pitch from the same distance. I take the same swing every time, not varying it according to the length of the shot. I vary the distance I want the ball to go by taking less sand for a longer shot. *Assuming that the sand is normal, I hit from one to three inches behind the ball; one inch on a long trap shot, three inches on a shorter one.* Trap shots are one situation in which I discard the dictum about keeping your eye on the ball. Instead, I look at a spot behind the ball which I select at the address. It requires some mental discipline and a good deal of concentration to focus on the spot and not the ball, but this should come with practice and actual experience on the course. This simplified technique of swinging the same way on all trap shots within 20 yards of the pin has helped my own trap play a lot and has also helped my pupils considerably. I have tried other techniques in teaching trap play, but I know this one is the soundest. I have found that in selecting the spot you want to hit behind the ball it helps to pick out a pebble as a guide. In my lessons, I place a wooden tee behind the ball or draw a line behind it. Using these guides as an aid, I then have my pupils try to execute the shot under my guidance. Naturally, they should continue the exercise on their own. One final note: by all means, use a sand-iron in playing a trap shot. Do not make the mistake of using a pitching wedge.

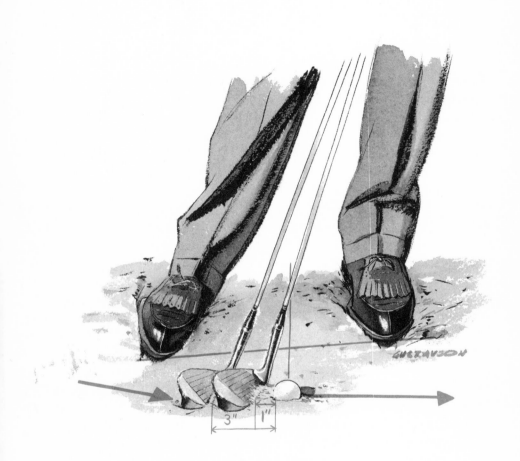

4. TRAP SHOTS
UNDER POOR CONDITIONS

By Jackson Bradley, PGA

River Oaks Country Club

Houston, Texas

PLAYING A BURIED BALL FROM SAND

Let us now consider a foul-weather problem—hitting the ball out of a wet sand trap. If the ball is sitting cleanly on the wet sand, it is treated like any normal lie in the trap.

The buried ball in a wet sand trap constitutes an entirely different problem. Place your feet so the ball is in the center of your stance. The club blade is held square or even slightly closed, while the stance is slightly open.

The position of the club over a clean lie suggests that we let the sand club work naturally, bounding down about one to two inches behind the ball, creating considerable back spin.

But the buried ball leaves the trap with a spinless action, followed by a considerable amount of run on the green. In playing the buried lie, keep the feet firmly planted in the sand. The backswing is quite strong, yet there is a minimum of motion. The left arm is the control factor in this shot as in all full shots. The *left* arm creates the force and must be used if any degree of proficiency is to be attained. In playing buried lies from wet sand, you must shock the ball loose with a solid downward stroke. You can best achieve this by strong use of the left arm and left leg. "Down and through" is the uppermost thought for this shot. The club should strike about one inch behind the ball. No effort is ever made to help the ball up. Note that the follow-through is quite short because the major force is expended in the descending blow and the initial thrust of the swing through the ball. As in all shots from buried lies, I plan on the ball running a good deal.

60

EXPLODING OUT OF WET SAND

In the explosion shot, or what we might call a sort of blast-and-run shot, as illustrated, I addressed the ball with the thought that it would run about halfway to the hole. With this in mind, I tried to place the ball just over the edge of the sand trap and on the edge of the putting surface. As it happened, that's exactly where the ball landed when these photos were taken. Momentum rolled the ball from there to the hole.

CHIPPING FROM THE TRAP

This photo illustrates a really sloppy lie—a buried ball in wet sand on the edge of casual water. When you have a shot like this, it is almost always correct to chip the ball out of the trap. The important thing here is to *hit the ball first*. As in all chip shots, I put more weight on my left leg. In the particular shot shown, I planned to put a little cut on the ball, so I have opened my stance where my body is facing the hole slightly. In a similar situation, except where the ball is sitting cleanly, you would be wise to play the ball off the surface of the sand as if it were on the fairway. The long semi-blast is really a gamble. However, if the pin is located close to the trap you have no choice but to use your sand club. Be certain, in this shot, that you strike down firmly under the ball. In wet, packed sand the club bounces up and out *fast,* causing inexperienced players to skull the ball.

THE BUNKER SHOT

By Gene Sarazen

Germantown, New York

The bunker shot is one shot I ought to know how to play. I invented both the club and the stroke to go with it. *Most people make the mistake of breaking their wrists when they try to execute a shot out of sand. Actually, the clubhead should be picked up with both hands together.* Executed properly, the ball should come out of the sand very slowly, because there is no flip of the wrists. By consciously using your wrists, you lose control of the ball. Remember: pick the club up, don't swing it back. And use a three-quarter swing. If you fear sand—as most players do—overcome your fear by practicing the method of the shot. Keep in mind that it definitely cannot be played with a nine-iron. You need the raised sole of a sand-iron in order to bring off the shot properly. As an indication of just how valuable the shot can be to you, it is estimated that the sand-iron has lopped off six to eight strokes in 72 holes for tournament players.

THE SLOW-MOTION TRAP SHOT

By Barbara Romack

Sacramento, California

What is it that gives a golfer the most difficulty in getting out of a trap? Nothing but fear and tension. The trap shot is really no more difficult than any other shot in golf. It's just that people think it is. When we are afraid of a shot, we tighten up. The first thing that happens is that we swing too quickly. Golfers in traps just can't wait to get out of them, and their rushed swings reflect this feeling. To counteract the tendency to swing too fast, deliberately swing as slowly as you can. With an open stance, play the ball opposite the left heel and open the blade quite a bit. Face slightly to the left of the hole, as the shot will fly a little to the right from such an address. Swing as slowly as possible, breaking your wrists abruptly at the start of the backswing. Hit very slowly under the ball and then on through up to a good finish. *The whole shot is played as in slow motion, from start to finish.* This may sound and feel foreign to you at first. But if you practice it for a while, you will work into that very slow tempo which minimizes tension and gives the greatest degree of control.

THE EXPLOSION SHOT

By Cary Middlecoff

Memphis, Tennessee

Few prospects are viewed with more distaste by golfers than a buried ball in a sand trap. When faced with such a shot, most people yank their sand-wedge from the bag, stomp into the bunker, and then whack at the ball with all their might, leaving the success of the shot largely to luck. Actually, exploding a ball that has been buried in sand requires not nearly so much power as you might think. All you need to bring off the shot is a little professional trick that will ignite the explosion for you. *Close the face of your wedge, then bury it behind the ball.* This, I know, is contrary to the usual technique of the trap shot, but it is a license you can take under the circumstances. By laying the face of your wedge open, as you should on normal trap shots, you are nullifying the effect of the front edge of the blade. By closing the face, however, you permit the blade to dig into the ground. As a result, the ball will pop out of the sand with surprisingly little effort. In fact, you will need not nearly as much follow-through to execute the explosion as you do when cutting the ball from a normal lie.

CUTTING THE BALL FROM SAND

By Al Besselink

Grossinger, New York

The trap shot ought to be the easiest shot in golf—you don't even have to hit the ball! Properly played, the trap shot is literally "missed." The ball is addressed with the face of the wedge laid wide open, so that the front edge acts as a knife blade. Then, you strike the sand at a spot several inches behind the ball. In short, you "cut" the shot. Sounds easy, but the fact of the matter is that even pros are sometimes afraid they can't properly cut the ball. It's one thing to hit a ball, but it's another matter altogether to *miss* it—properly, that is. On the circuit, for this reason, you sometimes hear the trap shot referred to as "the gut shot." Because, strictly speaking, it is a shot that requires more nerve than skill. Understandably, most amateurs are scared half to death of the trap shot. But once they overcome this fear, they are usually amazed at how really uncomplicated the shot is. To help you overcome your fear, *imagine that the front edge of your wedge is a knife blade and that running vertically through the spot behind the ball is a strand of rope.* With this picture in mind, you will soon discover that cutting a ball from sand is not much different (nor much harder) than cutting rope with a knife. Most people, I'll bet, can get the analogy in three shots or less.

PITCHING OUT OF SAND

By Johnny Farrell

Springfield, New Jersey

A ball can be hit cleanly from a trap when the sand is wet or very firm. You should not try it when the sand is dry and fluffy. This type of shot calls for an eight- or nine-iron, never a wedge. If the pin is back quite a way, use your eight-iron so the ball will run. Take an open stance with your weight just a little toward the left side. Hold your hands a little forward, too, and play the ball off your left heel. At the address, you should strive for a relaxed feeling in your forearms, especially the right one, since this is where most tension develops. On the backswing, break your wrists less than when exploding from a trap. *Hit the ball first—not the sand— with both your forearms and your wrists.* The shot is played, really, in practically the same way as a chip shot off the fairway, even to the extent of taking a slight divot. As a matter of fact, a good mental approach is to pretend that there *is* grass under you.

CUSHIONING THE SAND SHOT

By Olin Dutra

Rialto, California

Few golfers have adequate knowledge of the trap shot, nor do they practice it sufficiently. *The ball should be lined up with the left instep, because it is necessary that the wedge strike the sand about two inches behind the ball in order to create a cushion of sand between the ball and blade.* The stance should be extremely open; that is, the right foot should be well in advance of the left. The blade should be laid well back in order to assure sufficient backspin. To assure a cutting motion in the swing, the clubhead should be taken back outside the line of flight. The player's head must remain motionless until after impact.

THE CUT SHOT

By Sam Snead

White Sulphur Springs, West Virginia

In playing the trap shot, the average player positions the ball too far back toward the right foot. He should position the ball opposite the left heel. His stance should be slightly open and his feet about a foot apart. This open stance makes it easier for him to take the sand-iron back to the outside, the way he should. Essentially, then, the trap shot becomes a cut shot. *The sand-iron is picked up more abruptly than normal, and then cut across the desired line of flight on the follow-through.* This abruptness, of course, only applies to shorter trap shots. On longer recoveries from sand, your backswing should be more like that of a normal wedge, although the clubhead is still taken back toward the outside.

5. DEVELOPMENT OF THE SAND WEDGE

By Gene Sarazen

Necessity is the mother of invention, so the cliché goes, and it was necessity that compelled me to invent the sand-iron almost 30 years ago.

In 1931 I was intent on winning a British Open and also copping another National Open. Taking stock of my game, I realized that I was throwing away championships always because of one disastrous stroke in the course of 72 holes. And almost invariably this disastrous stroke could be traced back to a sloppily played trap shot that cost me a double-bogey, if not a worse score.

Plainly, something drastic had to be done to improve my bunker play. That something came to me, strangely enough, while taking flying lessons in Florida that winter. I was observing the action of the tail fins in making the plane go up or down. Perhaps, I thought, a "tail fin" on a niblick would help me to put quick loft on a trap shot. At any rate, I could hardly wait to get the plane back on the ground to see if some sort of a flange could be attached to a club that would serve the purpose of generating pronounced loft. I wanted to make myself a club that would drive the ball up as I drove the clubhead down. When a pilot wants to take off, he doesn't raise the tail of his plane, he lowers it. And so I wanted to lower the "tail," or sole, of my niblick to produce a club whose face would come up from the sand as the sole made contact with the sand.

At a machine shop in New Port Richey, where I was living, I had thick globs of solder attached to the underside of my niblick, to which I had added a few extra degrees of loft. The local golf course wasn't a very good one, but it did have one excellent bunker, right behind my house. I tried out my sand-iron there by hitting thousands of shots each week, making adjustments back in the machine shop and testing the improvement until I had the sand-iron perfected. Eventually, I felt confident of getting the ball within ten feet of the flagstick from any trap, regardless of the lie. And so the sand-iron was born.

I knew the club was revolutionary, so much so that I was scared to show it to anybody. I hid the head of it by placing the club upside-down in my bag while I was playing and by taking it home with me at night.

The first successful test of the sand-iron came at Prince's, in Kent, England, where I won the British Open that following spring, in 1932. Soon afterwards, I won my second Open, at Fresh Meadow, on Long Island. Thinking back, I cannot recall an instance in which I did not get down in two from a trap. In short, I won both those championships with the sand-iron.

The first thing you have to do in order to use the sand-iron is to take a lesson in its technique from your local pro. The technique of it is so utterly different from the technique of other irons that you are unlikely to find the secret through experimentation alone. You don't swing the clubhead. You pick it up with the hands and then drop it behind the ball. The clubhead is taken back outside the line of flight and then flicked down behind the ball, not too unlike the way you would swing an axe when chopping a tree.

And, above all, the wrists remain "unbroken" throughout the stroke. By "breaking" the wrists, you almost certainly will either top the ball or hit way behind it, resulting in one of those disastrous double-bogeys which the sand-iron was specifically designed to overcome.

GOLF EXTRA: HOW TO PROFIT FROM PRACTICE

By Mike Turnesa

I was recently asked if the old adage "practice makes perfect" holds good in golf. I could only give a qualified yes.

If a player knows what he is doing wrong and works along the proper corrective lines then, of course, he is going to reap the benefit. On the other hand, there is a great deal of wasted energy expended on the practice tee by players who go out there with their heads full of well-meaning, but misguided suggestions from fellow players whose knowledge of the theory of golf is just as flimsy as their own. They experiment by trying to correct one fault with another and never give themselves a chance to develop a smooth, well-grooved swing.

It is human nature to offer unsolicited advice, and nowhere is it more evident than on the golf course. A man hits a poor shot and all three fellow players have their own theories why. The misguided player gullibly swallows the proffered advice only to get himself deeper into the mire.

Though this advice is, on the whole, offered in good faith, more often than not it turns out to be backhanded gamesmanship. So, if you value the standard you have attained and don't want to take a retrograde step, close your ears even to your best friend on the golf course and seek the advice of your pro.

The average golfer, who has reached a reasonable degree of proficiency, seldom develops more than one fault if he suddenly loses form, and it is usually very basic—a slight change of grip, or stance out of alignment. If he would go straight to his pro and have a check-up, he could save himself a great deal of anguish and maybe weeks of bad play. Your pro is there to help you; it's his job. Many golfers have the quaint idea that they shouldn't bother a pro just as they shouldn't bother a doctor unless there is something seriously wrong. By that time it may be a long and arduous road back to recovery.

So, point number one, don't practice your faults. Have a check-up and start to practice along the right lines. Let's face it! Even the pros themselves take lessons.

Now we come to point number two—when should you practice? And here it depends on what you wish to accomplish.

Certainly you should limber up before you go out to play to tune up your muscles and get rid of any tension. It is an excellent idea to keep a weighted training club handy to swing before you start. Not only does this loosen you up, but it is invaluable during the winter months for keeping in practice when you can't get out to play. If you don't possess a training club, you can buy a weighted head cover from the pro shop, which serves the same purpose. Limbering up before you play may save you several strokes on the front nine.

Don't practice when you're feeling tired; it'll do you more harm than good. By all means go out and practice after your round, but take a breather first. Quit when you feel you are really in the groove and hitting the ball well. Even if you go fresh to the practice tee, an hour's practice is ample. After that you will get arm weary and undo the good you have done your game.

The longer handicap player, having a greater margin for improvement, can show greater dividends from practice, but, conversely, the low handicap golfer's swing is much more finely grooved and the slightest discrepancy is more likely to manifest itself. So, you see, practice is for everyone, even if it is merely to maintain your present standard.

Probably the cause of more bad play than any other is an incorrect grip. Though the grip of first-class players may vary slightly according to whether they swing upright or flat, or whether they hook or fade, the difference is very slight. In the longer handicap player, however, it may vary to a very great extent, and the more unorthodox it is, the greater the margin for error.

I do sincerely advocate that anyone seriously wishing to improve his game should check on his grip and work hard to bring it within the accepted tolerance. Even a slight change of grip can feel very awkward, and it takes time to adjust to it, so any major change can only be accomplished by degrees.

When making any radical change in your game it is better to stick to the practice tee than to go out on the course. When you hit a few poor shots on the practice tee it doesn't matter, but with a card and pencil the temptation to revert to the old method is too strong and may set you right back where you were.

Practice is not merely a routine of hitting ball after ball. It has a definite purpose and needs careful thought and planning. I have frequently seen golfers stride over to the practice tee with a couple of woods and maybe hit a couple of hundred balls either teed up or nudged onto the top of the most luscious tuft of grass. It may help their driving, and they may be able to hit an adequate three- or four-wood off the fairway from a good lie, but golf is more subtle than that. Let's say they find a poor lie off their drive so they hit their second into a trap. They then take three or four to get out. Why? Because they don't have the knowhow. They have never practiced the stroke-saving shots.

Bunker play costs the longer handicap player more strokes than any other facet of his game, yet a lesson on trap shots and a few practice sessions devoted to this alone would probably have him master of the shot in a matter of weeks.

Trap shots are but one of the trouble shots that golfers neglect. Seldom have I seen players drop a bag of balls in the rough, yet how often do they drive into it? Do they practice from uphill, downhill and sidehill stances? No, yet all these shots call for different techniques. No one can be a complete golfer until he has mastered all golf's many contingencies, but the incongruity of it all is that it is the longer handicap player who is more likely to encounter all the trouble spots.

When you start to practice, always have a target to aim at. It can be your ball bag or a handkerchief on the shorter shots, or the flagstick itself if you are practicing from a trap. On the longer shots you can choose a distant tree or any other suitable landmark. If you find you are pushing them out or hitting them left of target, lay a club along the line of flight and check your stance. Lay another at right angles to correct the position of the ball in relation to your feet. Incorrect alignment is one of the most common faults in golf. It is easy to fall into, but just as easy to spot and cure.

Always start your practice sessions with the precision clubs, the short-irons, which call for greater accuracy and more delicate touch, and work up to the longer clubs. This will develop your hand action and make you more conscious of the feel of the clubhead.

I have purposely left any reference to putting practice to the end. This is a highly individual matter because you can find just as good putters among the 90 and 100 shooters as those who break 80. However, if you do run into putting troubles you can take it for granted that you are breaking one of the basic rules and should seek professional advice. It is essential that you cultivate a smooth, unflurried putting stroke, and adequate practice can do much to improve your touch and also to boost your confidence.

Two further points. Rather have half a bagful of good practice balls than a bagful of duds. You cannot get the feel of a good shot with old, motheaten monstrosities. Golf faults are real enough without imagining others through the fault of the ball. And lastly, don't shop around for a teacher. Pick a pro and stick to him. A golf pro gets to know you and your game. Consult him when necessary and then practice what he preaches.

There is no short cut to good golf. It has taken the top pros and amateurs years of hard work and concentrated application on the practice tee to streamline their swing and master every shot. The percentage of players who aspire to that standard, of course, is negligible, but everything is relative and there is hardly a golfer alive who does not cherish dreams of lowering his handicap.

You don't improve merely by playing round after round, but your scores will reflect the time and effort profitably spent on the practice tee.

PART III: CHIP SHOTS

During a tense moment around the green, Doug Sanders was carefully surveying every blade of grass between the cup and the tough chip shot that he was about to execute. As he returned to the ball, he noticed a clergyman standing in the gallery.

"Would you like to play this for me, Father?" Sanders asked.

"Doug, you play it and I'll pray it," the Father replied.

Together, they knocked the ball stiff to the pin for one putt.

6. ABOUT CHIPPING

By Art Wall, Jr.

Several years ago, golf instructors taught two basic grips, the overlapping and the interlocking. Today, a third grip, the unlapping, is gaining more stature and may soon pass the interlocking as the second most popular. I have used this unlapping, or ten-finger, grip since I began playing golf and have found that it gives me additional power as well as more flexible wrist action. When I hit chip shots, I always have a good firm ten-finger grip on the club.

Firmness, in my opinion, is one of the most important fundamentals of good chipping. Since hitting a firm chip stems primarily from hand action, I make it a point to apply a little extra pressure on the grip with the last three fingers of my left hand and the thumb and forefinger of my right hand. This gives me a top-to-bottom firmness in my grip.

Chipping from the apron with a level lie, I play the ball off my right heel from a slightly open stance. My feet are about six inches apart and I keep slightly more weight on my left side throughout the shot. With my hands ahead of the ball at the address, it helps me to hit down on the ball crisply rather than try to scoop it up.

As I take the club back, I try to keep the clubface square to the ball at all times. (With long chip shots, this becomes particularly difficult and you should let the wrists roll naturally rather than try to force a square line.) I concentrate on keeping the back of my left hand facing the intended line of flight. This action will keep the blade square to the ball.

The firmness clearly comes into play on the downswing. Leading with the back of my left hand and the palm of my right, my hands are ahead of the clubhead at impact and the ball is hit crisply with a descending blow to prevent a scoop or flip.

In addition to the normal chip shot from the apron, there are several other types of shots which require a slight change in tactics and approach.

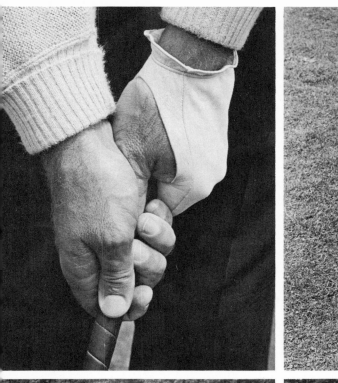

On uphill chips, I play the ball off the right foot, mainly because I want to hit the ball as solidly as possible. The change in tactics with this shot concerns the selection of the proper club. If you would use a six-iron from a level lie, use a five when the chip is uphill. The incline will add loft to the ball to the extent that a five-iron shot will behave like a six or even a seven-iron.

Downhill chip shots require the opposite approach on two counts. First, less club should be used than under normal conditions. I would use a seven- or eight-iron from a spot which would call for a six-iron on a level lie. Second, I play the ball off the left heel. Since the green is sloping downhill, I don't want to hit the ball firmly at all. Instead, I want to drop it onto the green softly. This type of chip closely resembles the lob shot which is by far the most difficult to execute of all shots around the green.

The lob shot should be used only when it is absolutely necessary because of its high degree of difficulty. I use this shot whenever I have to clear an obstacle such as a trap, a mound or hardpan surface. As with the downhill chip, you want to land on the green as softly as possible so that the ball will not roll too far or too hard. To play this lob, I open the face of the club, generally the wedge, and play the ball off my left heel. The difficulty of the shot comes from the fact that the ball must be hit with plenty of wrist action. This requires a lot of right hand and an extremely delicate touch. If you miss the shot by a fraction of an inch, chances are you'll either skull the ball across the green or drop it short. Unless you have the time and patience to practice this shot, I strongly recommend that you simply try to get the ball on the green as safely as possible and forget about floating it up to the pin.

Concerning the hit-and-run aspects of the chip shot, I prefer to let the ball run about two-thirds of the way toward the cup after it lands on the green. Naturally there are times when this is not possible—or preferred. For example, when you happen to be about 15 feet off the green and the hole is only ten feet from the apron, this certainly could not apply. In this situation, hitting the ball on the very edge of the green and letting it run all the way would be the best plan. Sometimes, I will run a ball only one-third of the way, letting the carry take up two-thirds of the distance. This I do when there is a rise in the green or rough spots to carry over.

To summarize, let me again stress firmness with the chip shot. Applying proper finger pressure and leading the downswing with the back of the left hand and the palm of the right hand will help achieve this. Analyze the chipping—and putting—surface carefully before selecting your club and use the lob shot only when there appears to be no other suitable alternative.

THE CHIPPING GRIP

By Walter Hagen

Traverse City, Michigan

Since most of us miss more greens than we hit—and I was no exception to this rule even when I was at my peak—we know how important it is to be sharp with our chips. Chipping is primarily a matter of touch. To illustrate, notice that your chips are seldom more than a foot or so off line. Thus, if you could chip the ball hole-high every time, you would never have a putt of more than a foot or so in length. The point, then, is to stop the ball as nearly hole-high as possible. And that takes touch. *Now, touch originates in the right hand, and I found that I could enhance this right-hand touch by letting the right hand play the predominant role in the shot. I did this by employing the reverse-overlapping grip with my chips, just as I did with my putts.* By reverse-overlap, I mean that the index finger of my left hand overlapped the little finger and ring finger of my right—the reverse of the usual overlapping grip.

JUDGING CHIPS

By Marty Furgol

Coghill, Illinois

In making a chip shot, I concentrate on taking the clubface away from the ball straightaway and hooding it on the backswing. Coming down on the ball, I open the face. At impact the clubface is square to the ball and I try to hit the ball just a little bit on the downstroke. This imparts a little backspin to the shot. In hitting a chip, I keep my feet together, weight slightly forward, hands more or less directly over the ball at address. My stance is open. On shorter chips, I use almost no wrist break. On the longer chips, I use more wrist break. *The hooding and opening I do when I hit a chip might be termed a sort of reverse pronation. I use it because it gives me the kind of spin I want and a good release at impact.* The eight-iron is my pet club for chipping. When the pressure is on and I'm not certain of the texture or hardness of the green, I use the eight-iron, because it gives me a good combination of pitch and roll. If I have a 20-foot chip with an eight-iron, I loft the ball half the distance and let it roll the other half.

SIMPLIFYING THE CHIP

By Bobby Jones

Atlanta, Georgia

I think it is a bad idea to use one club for all kinds of chip shots and short run-ups. Familiarity with the implement, of course, has its advantages, but it is practically impossible to secure a club which is effective from all distances and over all conditions of turf and terrain. *It is far better to be able to play the shot with any club which may be indicated by the shot at hand, so that the proportion of pitch and run may be accommodated to any position of the ball or hole with respect to the edge of the putting surface.* Except upon extraordinary occasions, I like to employ the club which will permit me, using a straightforward stroke, to pitch the ball just to the edge of the putting surface. For example, if my ball lay ten feet off the green, with the hole 30 feet from the edge, I would play a seven-iron, whereas if the ball lay only three feet off the green, I would use a four-iron. A great many players employ successfully what is known as "drag" on the chip. This is done by opening the clubface slightly and striking a sharp blow at the bottom of the ball. This is a refinement, however, which adds unnecessarily to the difficulties of the shot. It appears to me much simpler, if spin is needed for, say, a five-iron, to play a straightforward shot with either the eight-iron or nine-iron.

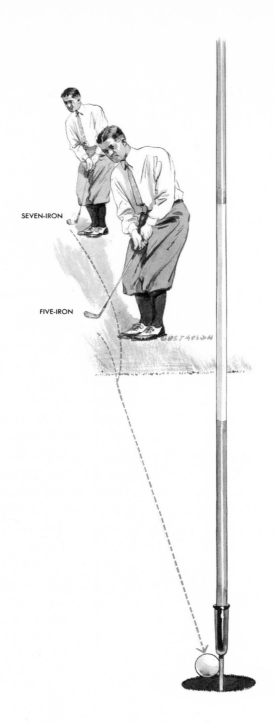

THE ART OF CHIPPING

By Don Fairfield

Casey, Illinois

As nearly everyone who follows or plays golf knows, the average and higher handicap player loses most of his shots on and around the greens. Faulty chipping is a major cause of much of this waste. *One thing that's been extremely helpful to me in chipping—and I've had success with this in teaching, too—is the practice of keeping the club I'm chipping with close to the ground on the backswing, downswing and follow-through. I try to make my chipping stroke as much like my putting stroke as possible.* Time and again I've seen golfers throw shots away by picking the club up too abruptly on chip shots. This chopping action causes them to hit the chip fat or to top it. The average player falls prey to another fault in chipping. This flaw is selecting the wrong club. In general, average players tend to select clubs with too much loft for chip shots. They pick a number eight- or a number nine-iron quite often. With these clubs, you'll get less roll, more backspin and less control. In my opinion, the main idea in chipping is to get the ball to roll. You can do this much more readily with a number five-, six- or seven-iron than with a more lofted club. My favorite for chipping is the number six-iron. With rare exceptions, it is best to land your chip on the green, not in the fringe. Only constant practice and play will enable a person to learn just how hard to hit chips in order to get best results. I recommend, for chip shots, standing with the feet close together, the weight evenly distributed and the hands slightly ahead of the ball at address. I play the ball opposite the center of my stance. I think it best to hit the ball very close to the bottom of the arc. Catching the ball too much on the downswing will impart too much backspin. For best results, it's advisable to choke up about three or four inches on the grip. This makes possible greater control of the club by the hands. The chip shot should be mainly a hands and arms shot. There should be no body motion at all.

96

AVOIDING FLUBBED CHIPS

By Gordon Jones

Atlantis, Florida

Two principles I try to keep in mind when chipping are to keep my weight mainly on my left side and to employ very little wrist-break. *Why keep the weight mainly on the left side? Because, in this position, you'll find that the hands are ahead of the ball at impact, thus insuring a more consistent stroke and avoiding deceleration of the clubhead during the downswing. By cutting down on your wrist-break, you will eliminate some motion in the swing and cut your chances of making an error.* The more simplified the swing, of course, the less chance there is of flubbing the shot. When using very little wrist action in chipping, about the worst you can do is hit the ball "thin," as we say. In chipping, I try to take the clubhead back straightaway and bring it down through the ball the same way. And here's another thought to bear in mind! Always try to make the shot as simple as possible. The big mistake many amateurs make is trying to make the shot harder by using a club that's too lofted. Of course, the club you should use depends on the lie of the ball, the amount of turf you must chip the ball over, and how much green there is between the edge of the green and the cup. Generally speaking, I would suggest a five- or a six-iron. But refrain from using a lofted club unless the situation demands one.

MY CHIPPING SECRET

By Ernie Vossler

Midland, Texas

Inasmuch as I am from West Texas, it was very important that I learn the best chip shot for windy days. Most golfers use too much loft when pitching and chipping, both with and against wind. I almost never use an eight- or a nine-iron or wedge when chipping. When chipping into the wind, I use the four-, five- and six-irons almost entirely, staying away from more lofted clubs. You must strike the ball more firmly than on comparatively windless days. *I usually use two clubs less chipping with the wind than against it.* In other words, assuming the same type of shot, I would use a five-iron against the wind and a seven-iron with it. With the wind, I usually employ a five-, six- or seven-iron. Of course, the degree of loft would be determined by the amount of grass the ball would have to carry. I always try to pick out a spot on the green beyond the fringe and attempt to land the ball there. I do this to preclude the possibility of getting a bad bounce from the often unpredictable fringe. If you limit your club selection on chips, eliminating the more lofted clubs, you are almost certain to develop a greater degree of consistency in chipping. The trajectory of the shots won't vary so much and you'll be better able to estimate the amount of run you'll get once the ball strikes the green.

CHIPPING MADE EASY

By Jim Ferrier

Burbank, California

My experience in pro-amateur tournaments and as a head professional, has convinced me that the average player misses at least half or more of the greens in a round, and is a bad chipper. I think the major reason he is a bad chipper is because he doesn't pick the right club. His common mistake is to pick the pitching wedge regardless of lie or position. It seems to me the average player over-uses the wedge anyway. The basic stroke for pitching and chipping is similar, the only difference being the club used. In chipping I always try to take a club that will land the ball on the green so the ball will roll smoothly to the cup, not just hope that it will. I try to use as little loft as possible because the probability of error increases as more loft is employed. You'll note that most good professionals try to keep the ball as close as possible to the ground when chipping and pitching. They seek simplification of the shot, want to avoid throwing the ball up in the air. *Always try to picture the shot before you hit, planning where you want the ball to land. Failure to visualize a shot before it is played is one of the most salient shortcomings of most amateur players.* For bad lies on chip shots I'd advise playing the ball about three inches farther back toward the right foot than usual so you'll catch it on the downstroke and get it out of the bad lie.

102

7. THE SHORT GAME

By Peggy Kirk Bell, LPGA

Pine Needles Lodge

Southern Pines, North Carolina

Conclusive proof has finally been added to the long-held belief that women golfers can compete favorably with the men on and around the greens. Playing on par-3 courses, the women established a 2-0 record against the finest men professionals in 1961.

I, like so many others, have always felt that the strongest part of a woman's game is in her pitching, chipping and putting. Since the women generally can't keep up with the men on the tee, it is around the green that they have their biggest chance to excel. Victories by Louise Suggs and the team of Mickey Wright and Barbara Romack have clearly demonstrated this point.

With all three shots, it is my opinion that the tight grip has always been the enemy of "touch" near the greens. Keeping a firm—but not tight—grip on the club, you'll find a surprising improvement in accuracy. Now, let's consider some of the short shots that will shorten the handicap.

On uphill approach shots close to the green, try to avoid using the wedge and nine-iron. The uphill slope increases the pitch of the club and you'll hit the ball higher than usual and short of your target. Sometimes you'll even end up short of the green. Use the seven- or eight-iron on the uphill approaches. This will result in proper flight and distance.

On the longer pitches of 40 to 75 yards, the same general rules apply. Keep your weight over on the left side. You should play the ball off your right heel. In doing this, you'll hit the ball with a descending blow of the clubhead.

One common question that all golf instructors are asked by almost all

On uphill pitches, the ball is opposite the right heel, and the weight should be forward. With the left side firm at impact, the ball is hit with a descending blow.

In playing the "hit-and-run" chip shot, the hands are ahead of the ball at the address. Stance is open, and the ball is played in close to assure an upright swing.

lady golfers is: "How do you stop the ball on the green?" or: "Can you show me how to get backspin on the ball?" To do this you must cut across the ball, playing it off the left foot and hitting it hard. A ball will never "bite" unless you hit down on it.

Chip shots are those executed on the apron of the green or just off the apron. One type of chip shot is commonly called the "hit-and-run." With this shot, there is ample green to chip the ball and let it roll most of the way toward the hole.

I like to use a seven-iron for such a shot. Play the ball off the left heel. Open the stance and position the hands ahead of the ball. The weight should be forward on the left side. The feet should be close together.

It is a common fault for women to pull chip shots. The pulling is caused by playing the ball too far away from the body. When the ball is too far away, it makes the golfer bend at the waist too much. The ball should be played in close so that you can stand up and hit it without reaching. This position makes for better stroking and keener distance perception.

Grip down on the club and keep the clubhead low along the ground on the backswing. Use very little wrist in hitting into the ball. After the ball is lofted from the apron to the green, the ball should roll toward the hole like a putt.

One of the most common faults among women golfers is that they too often play the chip shot with most of their weight on the right foot. This will cause them to hit up, or scoop the shot. Don't try to lift the shot with the clubhead. Let the natural loft of the club do the work. One has to hit the shot with the weight on the left and hit through the ball. Then it will be impossible to scoop it on the chip.

On chip shots from thick grass near the green, take a comparatively loose grip. You'll get more control that way. Too firm a grip employed in rough or heavy grass may cause the ball to pop up. It may even cause the dreaded shank. The tight grip locks the wrists, causing the neck of the club to push through the ball rather than the clubface doing so.

Putting is one part of the game about which a golf instructor is hesitant about being positive. From my experience I have found many high handicap golfers have a "touch" on the greens that some of the touring pros would envy. The best putting stroke in the world would be useless without the "touch" or "feel" for putting.

Here are some basic fundamentals that I feel should help the golfer,

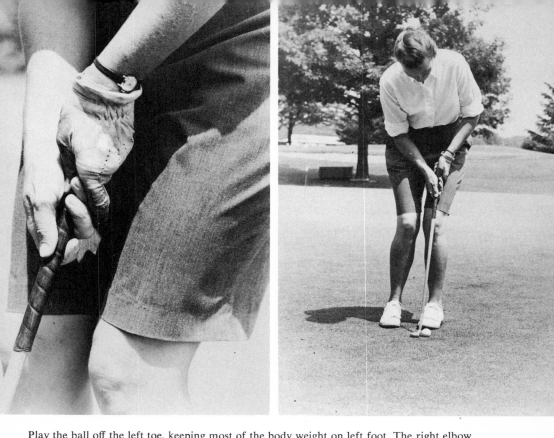

Play the ball off the left toe, keeping most of the body weight on left foot. The right elbow is close to the side as the left hand brings back the putter. The reverse-overlap grip enables the right hand to exercise more control over the putting stroke. The right hand taps the ball as both hands execute a complete follow-through.

whether she is a mediocre putter or a good one who is in a slump.

To begin with, I use the reverse overlapping grip. I put the right hand on the shaft and lay the left hand on the shaft with the left forefinger overlapping the right hand. Thus, the hands are very close together and the grip is soft, not tight. Arrange the hands so the thumbs are pointing straight down the shaft. The hands are away from the body a short way to allow them freedom of action. The right elbow should rest against the right hip.

Keep the weight on the left foot throughout the putting stroke. Play the ball off the left toe. I point the left toe in slighlty. This keeps the head and body motionless and helps prevent body turn, which results in pulling the putt to the left and pushing it to the right.

I believe in taking the putter back with the left hand and stroking forward with the right hand. In other words, on medium length or short putts the hands remain almost stationary. On the longer putts, you'll have to use arm movement in the stroke for distance. The amount of "arm" in the stroke will be according to your perception of the distance to be travelled from your ball position to the hole.

The forward stroke is accomplished by a smooth tap with the right hand. The follow-through is important. Continue the hands through the ball low to the ground on the line of roll to the cup.

I prefer a heavy, mallet-head putter which will do the work with less wrist and arm action. The heavy putter makes the follow-through of the stroke easier and more accurate. The mallet putter helps you stroke through the ball low and on line.

The wind is a larger factor in putting than most golfers realize. When putting with the wind, shorten the stroke, for the wind will push the ball along. When putting against the wind, lengthen the stroke. Make the appropriate adjustments for crosswind putting. The wind will definitely affect your putting on the greens. Remember that.

In this article I have tried to emphasize some of the ways in which women golfers can cut their scores around the greens. I'd like to summarize by listing the most important points from each of the three articles.

First, the width of the stance should be approximately the same as the width of the shoulders. Too wide a stance interferes with weight transfer and generally causes the body to sway. This is one of the most common faults among women golfers.

Second, the left side should dominate the backswing. Take the club away with the left shoulder, arm, hip and hand, making a swinging turn in one piece.

Third, maintain a firm—but never tight—grip on the club. A tight grip causes tension which can lead to practically anything but good results.

GOLF EXTRA: STRAIGHT SHOOTER

By John Gallagher

Illustrated by Joe Farris

Fairway Flanagan they call him, and he's running away with the club championship. Him and his hickory-shafted clubs. Irons of rust and woods with more nicks than a butcher's block. And does he ever play a ball that's perfectly round, somewhat white, unbroken of cover—does he? No, never. Not him. Not Fairway Flanagan.

The club referred to is Crow Flight Country Club. Naturally, it's not exclusive and none of us who play it are rich, least of all Fairway Flanagan. Mind you, we don't know that he's really poor. But how else can you account for a guy using equipment like he uses? Or dressing the way he does? His spikes have the baldest nubs I've ever seen. Moving up from there we come to his faded, flimsy, lavender slacks, which, it is rumored

around the clubhouse, are the same slacks Jimmy Demaret wore when he played in his first tournament. Fairway wears a tattered T-shirt and completes the ensemble with a sweat-stained visor that was white when Hoover was President.

Now, maybe you're asking—okay, Charley Benedict, so what do you have against this poor fellow?

I'll tell you. Yesterday, I played my semi-final round against Flanagan. Now, I've lost before, and I'll lose again, but to lose to a guy who plays like Flanagan is the next worst thing to losing your mind. For one thing, Flanagan can't hit a ball off the tee any farther than my wife, and Madge's best is about 180. But he's straight, see; he's incredibly straight. He has never, so help me, that guy has never wavered off line more than maybe a foot in all the time I've seen him play. And that's the thing that's galling, for I hit a long ball off the tee—average 260, sometimes with good roll edging up to almost 300. Granted, I do a lot of scrambling, but still I score good. That is, until I play Flanagan.

The guy unnerves me. Like yesterday. Time after time I'm out there from 80 to 100 yards ahead of him. Take the eleventh at Crow Flight. It's a flat, 400-yard par-four. Flanagan gets his ratty looking driver out and hits a blooper about 170. Then I come up and blast one that smokes and leaves me a wedge to the green. I'm a good 100 yards out beyond him;

more than that. Well, he goes to his ball, takes out his brassie, hits another one about 170. Again, straight as a trolley wire.

When I get to my ball, I decide to use a nine and I hit a beauty that's about seven feet from the cup. I'm there in two. Flanagan is still 50 yards off the green.

Well, now, who're you betting on? You'd say me, wouldn't you? Especially when you know that I sink those seven-footers with my eyes half closed. All right.

Flanagan hits his third shot. It's straight, like always, and the ball winds up about ten feet away. So he's lying 3, I'm 2 and it looks like my hole.

He asks for the flag to be taken out, which the caddie does, and then he lines up his putt. To watch Flanagan line up a putt is even more distracting than to watch him hit those straight bloopers of his. First of all, when you look at the crummy ball he's using, it's enough to make you sick. Cuts in it, and maybe a little lop-sided, and do you think he'd stop now and then to run it through the ball washer? Not him. Not Flanagan.

Well, can you guess what happens? He holes it, I two-putt and the hole is halved. From then on, I'm shot. After I watch his ball egg its wobbly way into the cup, brother, I just don't have it any more. He closes me out on the thirty-second. That was yesterday.

Today Flanagan is meeting Gerry Wilson, and Gerry is just about the best golfer I've ever seen at Crow Flight. He used to be a one-handicapper, but now he plays from scratch, and I'm telling you this is the guy to watch when the Amateur is played, and beyond that the Open. He's got such a sweet swing and how he can lay the clubhead against that ball! Gerry's only a kid and, personally, I think he'll be able to stand the gaff of 36 holes

112

much better than Flanagan. Fairway's about fifty-five, and what with the heat, plus his having played 32 holes yesterday, well, I don't think he's got a chance. Straight and all, luck and all, Flanagan's got to fall apart sometime.

Gerry wins the honor and he lines a steamer out that's long and true on this downhill, 380-yard par-four first.

"Nice shot, kiddo," Fairway assures him as he tees up his ball. Even though it hurts me to tell you, Flanagan looks his usual mess. The bald spikes and the cracked, unshined leather of the shoes, which is all I'm looking at because, frankly, I can't stand to take in the rest of him. After all, a lot of golfers from other courses are standing around the first tee to watch this club championship match. What must they think of Crow Flight when they see a sloppy guy like Flanagan?

Fairway hits his customary drive, fly-ball-to-center, and the crowd moves off the first tee. As we walk along I am thinking of that old but true saying as I look at calm, confident Gerry Wilson: Youth must be served.

Fairway's second shot falls just short of the green. Wilson lobs a wedge that grabs just beyond the flag and rolls back to within four feet for almost a gimme bird.

Flanagan takes out his putter, a club I shudder to see in his hands. Like his irons, it's rusty and hickory shafted, but in addition it seems to have a warp in it and, further, the leather grip has strings hanging from it. This last he could fix with some tape, but not him. Not Flanagan.

Flanagan lines up his putt. Here, I am thinking, is the secret of this guy's success. Give the devil his due, this guy has a sense of alignment that is uncanny.

People around the green, close to his decrepit looking ball, make remarks and you can hear some giggling from the girls as they see the crescent gash in this ball Flanagan is being so careful about.

It all stops, though, when he runs the ball right into the cup. The crowd applauds, Flanagan doffs his dirty visor, and Wilson, poor guy, takes two from four feet out. Flanagan is one-up as we go to the second tee.

Let's pause here now. I was going to give you a play-by-play, but when Gerry Wilson went eight down at the turn, I decided to come in and have a cool one and think things over.

What happened? How could such a fine golfer like this Wilson kid go sour? The news finally comes to me. Flanagan wins the match on the twenty-third. But even more disappointing is Wilson's threat never to play the game again.

Somehow, I make it to the presentation ceremony. I want to see what they're going to give Flanagan besides the cup. Of all things, it's a set of new irons and woods. Flanagan's eyes water when he accepts the gift—he's a kind of sentimental lout with it all. Then he makes a small speech and I get the impression he's going to run for public office.

I don't see Flanagan again for maybe two weeks. Then, one Sunday morning, when it looks like it's going to pour any minute but doesn't—you know the kind of day—he's on the first tee. No one else is there and he's practicing his swing. With the new clubs.

"Charley!" he says when I walk up, pulling my cart, "how about a round?"

Well, like I say, no one else is there. What have I to lose? Besides, it looks like rain and probably I won't have to be in his company for too many holes. "Okay," I tell him and he quickly tees off.

Right there on his first shot—a looping, screaming hook—the whole pattern of his play shows itself. He can't do with the new clubs what he's done with the old. Instead of being straight, he's a little longer; instead of being consistent, he's erratic.

At the end of nine—still no rain—I have him three down. I'm savoring the triumph when Flanagan excuses himself and goes to his locker, carrying the new clubs with him.

When he returns to the tenth tee—well, you guessed it—he has the old, beat-up sticks with him. To be honest about it, I am both appalled to see them again and a little nervous because the memory is still too fresh of what he's done to all of us with those sticks.

However, and this I still can't get over, Flanagan doesn't have the touch with the old clubs any more. No sir. He can't do a thing like he used to. He still hits the ball okay, but he has no idea where it's going. Somehow, he's lost it. The new clubs. That's what it is.

Otherwise, how would I wind up eight holes ahead of Fairway Flanagan?

Last time I saw Flanagan—the day after our match—is in a hardware store in town. He's standing with a new post-hole digger in hand by the register, waiting to pay the clerk. Somehow, I don't feel so unfriendly toward the guy, now that I've beaten him at last.

"Hi, Flanagan," I say. "Whacha doing with a post-hole digger?"

He looks at me, then the digger, and he says, "I'm going to dig me two holes. Two long, deep holes."

You know, he hasn't been back to Crow Flight since and I miss him. We all do. Straight shooters like Flanagan don't grow on trees.

Not even on hickories.

PART IV: PUTTING

After a fantastic round of putting in the 1957 Eastern Open, Tommy Bolt was holding court with the men of the press. One of the first questions asked was whether or not he was satisfied with his putting that day.

The answer was obviously yes, but Tommy, scratching his lantern jaw, fooled them all. "If I made every putt for the rest of my life," Bolt replied, "I still wouldn't be even."

8. PAUL RUNYAN EXPLAINS HIS THEORIES ON PUTTING

With Robert Joseph Allen

Roam any fairway where championship golf is played and you are apt to find it staked out with golfers who at one time or another have been influenced by the putting theories of Paul Runyan. Driving from Phoenix, Arizona, which is my bailiwick, to Lá Jolla, California, which is where Runyan holds forth these days, I couldn't help but see a startling parallel: the road to Runyan literally was paved with his disciples.

Several Cadillacs passed me on the way. Bob Goalby, one of the brighter new stars on the PGA tour, happened to be driving one of them. Had he ever taken any putting lessons from Runyan? "Of course Runyan has taught me," he replied. "How else would I have been able to win enough to pay for *that?*" he said, waving his hand at his fuchsia-colored Fleetwood.

I also encountered young Phil Rodgers, the National Intercollegiate champion in 1958. "How come you putt so well?" I asked this blond and bronzed young man who is built like a college shot-put champion.

"I always try to putt the way Paul Runyan taught me to," he answered.

It is generally known along the circuit that Gene Littler, one of the most consistent money winners on the tour, attributes his remarkable comeback of a couple of years ago to the teachings of Paul Runyan. Ask Littler if he ever took putting lessons from Runyan, as I did, and he will tell you, "Doesn't everyone?"

The Lá Jolla Country Club, where Runyan is head professional, sits in all of its dreamy green magnificence on top of a high cliff overlooking the ocean. While scouting him out, I came across the tall, lissome figure of Mickey Wright, who told me, "I have just left him. He has been giving my putting stroke another honing." Then with her eyes looking off in the distance, as though fixed on far-off triumphs yet to come, she drifted away.

Runyan, who during his heydey in the Thirties, won the PGA cham-

The Runyan putting grip, with the V's pointing almost to the hips, equalizes gripping power and minimizes wrist action.

pionship twice—the second time, in 1938, beating Sam Snead—was five times a member of the Ryder Cup team, won 50 sectional titles, and was known as "Little Poison" because of his small build, was in the pro shop when I finally caught up to him. I told him that, attracted by his renown as a savant of the elusive art of putting, I had come to inquire into his wondrous skill.

"I wasn't aware, Bob," he replied, "that I am a 'savant', as you put it, but it is true that I've had a certain amount of success with using and teaching the putter over a long period of years and I'm proud of the fact, that, by sticking to fundamentals, the kind of putting I practice and teach has helped many others. The system that I use for putting," he explained, "is based upon opinions of doctors, oculists, and successful tournament golfers. In regard to wood or iron shots on a practice tee, I have to know something about the person, his shape, form, how much he has played, and how well. But on a putting green a knowledge of those things in connection with the person taking a lesson is not necessary.

"When a person comes to me for a putting lesson, regardless of how good or poor a putter he is, I follow a set pattern based on the established fact that binocular vision is the *only* accurate vision we can possibly use in putting the ball on a straight line. 'Binocular vision' is what you see when you stand erect and look directly out in front of you. In this way the human eye can form a straight line, or can get an opinion of a straight line.

"Now, the next best vantage point from which the human eye can achieve binocular vision, or, in other words, a straight line, is a 90-degree angle either right or left. Thus, if a person keeps the line of his toes, hips, and shoulders exactly parallel to the direction that he wants to putt the

119

ball, he will have a sound putting position. I want my toes, or the toes of my pupils, lined up so that there is no line of demarcation at all between the line the putt is going to roll on and the line that they're placing their feet on. This is the position in which it is easiest to swing the putter in a parallel line back and forth, and anyone will readily understand that the art of putting a ball straight is merely to swing the club parallel with a line leading straight to the cup, with the clubface at right angles.

"Since the wrist has a tendency to pronate and supinate (pronation and supination are the acts of turning the palms—if they are up, they are in a supinated position; if they are downward, they are in a pronated position) it therefore follows that if you place your hands on the club so that your palms are in a neutral position, as you do in gripping clubs for long shots, your wrist can then turn approximately 90 degrees from either side of that position before they reach the state of block, or where they can't turn any more. Even though this position of the hands is desirable in the long shots in order to create power, we *don't* want it on short shots where power is not the object but where directional control and a sensitive touch is the aim. If you're putting, and you have any pronation and supination in the stroke, it's difficult to hit the ball straight.

"The correct thing to do is take hold of the putter first with your left arm bent slightly against your side so that the forearm is nearly horizontal. When you do this the palm of your left hand is facing upward in a vertical position. Then you let the shaft of the putter lie across the palm of that hand in an angular position, coming out of the fore part of the hand and the heel of the hand. Now bring the right hand up to that same position, with the right elbow lying against your body and the right forearm in a semi-horizontal position, the face of your right hand turned slightly upward. When you've taken hold of the club in this position, the V formed by thumb and first finger of both the left and right hand points toward their respective shoulders, or even a little below the shoulders, almost to the hips is even better.

"When you get your hands in this position, even if your wrists begin to work in a wristy manner, you're still not likely to have the base of the club diverted very much. However, I don't approve of a great deal of wrist motion in the stroke. I try to keep the wrist motion out.

"Whether a person uses a reverse overlap, an overlap, or a plain eight-finger grip, is of no major importance. You want to get approximately the same gripping power in each of the hands, and if you have a putter that has a much larger grip toward the upper end than it has at the lower end, then I'd suggest that you use a reverse overlap, so that the last three fingers of the left hand have about the same gripping strength on the larger surface at the top end as your right hand, which is farther down the shaft on the small of the surface. However, it's better to have a grip that doesn't have much taper to it, and then you may use a plain eight-fingered grip. But whether you use a plain eight-fingered grip, an overlapping grip, or a reverse overlap grip, be sure that the two V's formed by the thumb and first finger of each hand point sharply outward below the respective shoulders, or in other words, have the palms of the hands facing upwards slightly.

"You should bend over the ball in such a way as to cause your eyes to be directly over it, because the oculists have informed me that it's easier to see the straight putting line when your eyes are directly above the ball than it would be if they were on the outside of the putting line looking inward, or on the inside looking outward. You have a tendency to see a slightly curved line from either one of these two latter positions. Thus, it becomes evident that, to get their eyes directly above the ball, very tall people will generally need to be a little bit farther away from the ball when they bend their body over, than would be the case with a somewhat shorter person. But, at any rate, whatever your size or shape, you need to get your body bent over in such a way that your eyes are directly above the ball, position-wise.

"Now the next point is: Where do we want the ball in relationship to the feet in order to strike the ball most accurately? There are some fine instructors who believe that the ball should be hit on the downswing. There are others who believe it should be hit on the upswing. In my opinion, it should be hit just as the club has reached the very bottom of the arc of the swing and is swinging parallel to the earth, neither going up nor coming down, so that the ball starts along the green, immediately turning forward. If you hit it on the downswing it is likely to skid a few inches before starting to turn. If you hit it on the upswing it might hop a little as it first moves. It will obviously start with a forward roll most easily when you keep the blade of the putter at exactly a right angle to the ball and the intended line of the putt at the address position, and swing it back and through so that you come back to that exact position on impact with the ball.

"How can this best be accomplished? If you stand with your weight evenly balanced, and the ball slightly left of the center, you can then get your hands placed in such a way that the shaft of the club attains this right-angle position most easily. I beseech anyone who wants to putt soundly to keep the hands even with the back side of the ball in the address position and practice until they can hit the ball again with their hands exactly at that same line of scrimmage, so to speak. To accomplish this most easily, do we stroke it with the arms, the body, or a turn of the shoulders? In my opinion, the greatest amount of motion should come from the shoulder joint, rather than from the elbow joint or the wrist joint. In other words, I want my upper arm, my forearm and my putter to swing back as much as possible in a single unit, hitting the ball more or less as though you were going to hit it with your left elbow as you come through.

"After a person has achieved a good mechanical stroke, the next question is: What is the best type of putter? Putters should have some loft on the face of them, generally a loft of about four degrees if the putter is of normal depth, a tiny bit less if the putter is a very thin-bladed putter. The law of gravity being what it is, the ball has a tendency frequently to settle in a little depression, and a little loft on your putter will help overcome any jump or crooked bounce the ball might have as it comes out of such a depression, or any roughness of the green it encounters as it first starts. There's also the question of nap on the green. If you're using a putter with no loft at all, and you're hitting the ball against the nap it may have a tendency to spin it to one side or the other. Loft on a putter guards against this, too.

"Aluminum is about the best material that has been devised so far for a putter head—aluminum with preferably a small amount of lead in it. I'm not an expert on metals, but experience has taught me that a good aluminum putter has a deadening effect on the ball and you can tap it a little

Palms pointing upwards, eyes directly over ball, Runyan stresses the need for the elbow joints, wrists and putter to act as one unit.

firmer without the ball racing on you, and when you can tap it quite firmly, it is better in my opinion.

"Now let's turn to the weight of the putter. I believe the putter should be either light or heavy—not medium. If you have a very fine sense of touch, you can usually get very good results and perhaps do best with a light putter. If you're one of these big-handed, heavy-wristed men that do not have a delicate touch, then your best bet is to buy a putter that is very heavy.

"As to the materials in the shaft, I used a wood-shafted putter until about five years ago and always did very well with it. Then I decided that I would try steel as an experiment. I wanted to give it good long try until I was fully conversant with its advantages or disadvantages. A steel shaft has little or no torsion in it. Therefore, if you hit the ball off the center of the face of the steel-shafted club, it won't react to torsion forces to the same degree that would occur in wood. However, after testing steel shafts for some time, I'm now back to using wood, and I'm fairly well convinced that wood, despite its tendency to torsion a little, has advantages that out-weigh its disadvantages.

"As to the degree which a putter should be upright or flat, I believe that if a person happens to be one of those who has to stand quite close to the ball in order to get his vision directly above it for that 'binocular' vision I mentioned earlier, obviously he's going to have to use a fairly upright putter. If he's a very long-jointed person that has to bend over a good bit more in order to keep his vision in the proper place, he is going to want a putter a little bit flatter.

"The putter should have a rocker sole so that if you should happen to scuff the ground a little bit, it's not likely to twist or turn in your hand. A 'rocker sole' is one that curves from toe to heel and from side to side on the face. It gives it a sort of ball-bearing effect, which is a highly desirable thing to have in a putter so that if it does scuff the ground in the act of making the stroke, being curved on all bearing surfaces, it will ride through more accurately.

"Now I want to say something about the psychology of putting. You might say, 'Well, if a person has a good sound style, won't it naturally follow that his psychology in the matter is also sound?' But psychology differs from confidence a great deal. A person may be an extrovert, and have a good bit of confidence in himself, but if the psychology, or theory of putting that he's using, is not sound, then he's had it. For example, the 'never up, never in' theory of putting in regard to long putts is the most fallacious theory that I know of. There is no one in the world that I've ever seen that has a touch that is good enough to use the 'never up, never in' theory to advantage from greater than ten or 12 feet. If a person tries to hit a ball past the hole from 15, 20, 25, and 30 feet, he's more than liable to knock the ball by the hole so far that he's going to three-putt more frequently than one-putt.

"Few things can irritate me more than to be playing in a pro-amateur event with some good friend who's got about a 20-foot putt to make, and who, if he gets it down in two, is going to save us a stroke, because he gets a stroke on the hole. Then he hits it eight or ten feet by the hole and comes up with the classic remark, 'Well, I gave it a chance.' Actually, he gave it no doggoned chance at all!

"If a person were to hit his irons up to the green on a given day so that all of his putts were 20 feet or longer, he has had a *very* good putting day if he takes only 36 putts. Likely, he lagged the ball up to the hole intelligently, like a youngster does in big-ring marbles. If the marbles are in the center of the small ring line and he's required to taw from the big ring, he doesn't go for the marbles the first try, if he's sensible. He *lags* to the center ring and goes for them next time. Now that same thing is true with the longer putts. If you've got a long putt to make you should sensibly visualize the hole as a one-foot cup rather than a four and one-quarter-inch cup, and *lag* the ball up to that imaginary one-foot cup. Whether it stopped six inches short, or six inches right, six inches left, or six inches past, it's a good putt—it insures you a two-putt hole.

"In connection with the short putts of ten feet or under, provided they're not tricky downhill putts, then the theory of 'never up, never in' is a good one. Anyone with a reasonable amount of diligent practice and a putter that feels right in his hands can 'give it a chance' by risking passing the hole without passing it so far as to make three-putting a likelihood.

"Another thing in the psychology of putting, is when do you buy a new putter? Never buy a new putter when you're putting poorly—only buy a new putter when you're putting well, for then you're doing this because you sincerely feel that you have seen a putter that's a superior implement. But if you buy a new putter when you are putting badly, hoping that it's going to make a change in your putting, and it doesn't turn out right, *then* where are you? You've got nothing to go back to with confidence at all."

"Bobby Locke is generally rated the best putter of all time—do you think he is?" I asked Runyan.

Runyan "lags" his long putts, applies the "never up, never in" theory only on putts of less than ten feet. He favors an aluminum headed putter with a wooden shaft and wisely advises that you change your putter only when you are putting well.

"No, Horton Smith was," he replied. "Locke perfected his own style, which he believed in, and with complete confidence he could what I call 'brush' the ball into the hole with more success than most, whatever their style. Sarazen was one of the best putters I ever knew. He was the extrovert, cocky type of putter—in streaks he could beat either Bobby or Horton. On the days when Sarazen was good, he was wonderful, but on the days when he was bad, he was horrible. Incidentally, I've always believed that courageous, strong-willed people like Sarazen make the best putters.

"But the most dramatic and memorable putt of all time insofar as I am concerned," said Runyan, "occurred during an extra-hole match between Craig Wood and myself. It was only a nine-foot putt from the center of the green, and it had smooth sailing all the way to the cup, but it was the one that won me the 1934 PGA championship on the second hole of that play-off."

125

PICKING A PUTTER

By Fred Haas, Jr.

Metairie, Louisiana

Every golfer should determine which eye is his master, or dominant, eye.*
Inasmuch as putting essentially involves a 90-degree-angle alignment between the master eye, the putter-face and the cup, it follows that a "right-
eyed" person will more naturally be able to line up putts if he uses a
goose-necked putter. This type of putter curves back in the direction of a
90-degree angle between the right eye, the putter-face and the hole. *The
point I am trying to drive home here is that the master eye should be directly over the putter-face.* To get good results on the green, it is necessary
to eliminate as many compound angles as possible. The reason many golfers hit their putts solidly and do not sink them is that they are not lined up
properly. A right-eyed person should be careful, if using a goose-necked
putter, not to play the ball too far forward. This mistake leads to looking
at the putter-face from an angle and defeats the idea he is seeking. If a
goose-necked putter is better for the right-eyed person, then the converse
is true for a "left-eyed" person. A straight-necked putter would be better.
The main thing I am trying to stress is that you have to strive to maintain
as straight a line (or 90-degree angle) as possible between the master eye,
the putter-face and the cup. If you do, you'll find you'll get better results
on the green, because your natural alignment will be better.

---

* To determine the master eye, take a sheet of paper and punch a hole in it with a pencil.
Place a coin on the floor and, holding the paper at arm's length, look through the hole at
the coin—with both eyes open. Alternate shutting each eye. The one that sees the coin is
the master eye.

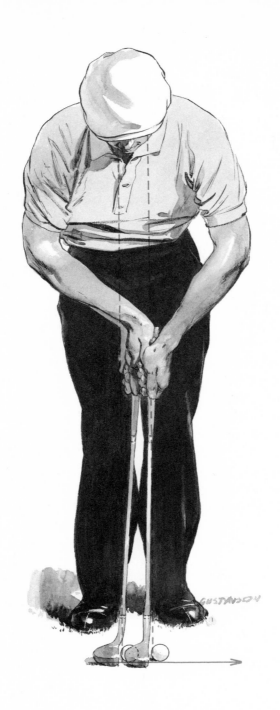

GRIPPING THE PUTTER PROPERLY

By Bob Watson

Elmsford, New York

The reverse overlap grip consists of lapping the left forefinger over the little finger of the right hand. The reverse overlap grip is one that has become very popular among many of our fine players today because it allows the player to comfortably place his left thumb directly on top of the shaft and square the palm and back of the left hand to the target. It also tends to throw the control pressure to the rear of the left hand. These three positions allow the left hand to hinge back and forth without losing control of the putter or without opening or closing the clubface. The reverse overlap grip allows you to place all fingers of the right hand on the putter shaft, thus allowing you to exert the most efficient control over the length and deftness of the stroke. It also makes it relatively easy to put the right thumb directly on top of the shaft and square up the palm and back of the right hand with the hole. With the normal overlap grip, only three fingers of the right hand are on the shaft and the player cannot generally have as much control over the stroke as he can with all four fingers on the shaft. *Simply, the reverse overlap grip sets up good positions of control with the left hand while it encourages good positions of feel and touch with the right.* At the same time these two functions are working together.

DEVELOPING A PUTTING STYLE

By Bill Collins

Baltimore, Maryland

In the last couple of years, I have gone from being one of the worst putters on the tour to one of the best. I think what helped me can help you. First, here's how I position myself over the ball. *I have the ball about nine inches opposite my left toe and my eyes over the ball. My hands are slightly ahead of the putter head, my feet about a foot apart, and my knees angled in toward one another in sort of a knock-kneed style, à la Arnold Palmer.* This knock-kneed style locks me into position, I feel. I try to contact the ball right in the center. In stroking the ball, I feel I am hitting down and I feel as if I were practice putting with a wedge. By hitting down slightly and contacting the ball in the center, I get good roll that helps the ball stay on line better. The fact that the ball is about nine inches opposite my left toe places it directly under my eyes, giving me a better view of the line. This position also encourages me to take the putter back inside and to stroke the putt from the inside. I address the ball with the heel of the putter, too. Once I've decided on the line, I forget about it.

9"

PLUMB-BOB PUTTING

By Al Geiberger

Studio City, California

The plumb-bob system of lining up putts is one in which the player uses his putter in the manner of a surveyor's instrument. I find it helpful because it gives me confidence in my having read the green correctly. It sort of corroborates my judgment on the greens. *In using the system, you must stand so that a straight line extends from your dominant eye to the ball and then on to the hole.* The other eye must be kept closed. *Your dominant eye is the eye which allows you to see one object superimposed over another in the same way both eyes can see the superimposition.* The putter should be held perpendicularly at arm's length with the thumb and forefinger gripping it at the bottom of the grip. It is best to stand from three to six feet back of the ball when lining up. As a rule, the shorter the putt, the closer you stand to the ball. Cover the ball with the lower part of the putter shaft and then run your dominant eye up the shaft. If the shaft covers the hole, the putt is straight. If the shaft falls to the left of the hole, the putt will break from left to right. If the shaft falls to the right of the hole, the putt will break from right to left. The system works best on putts from 15 feet or less.

132

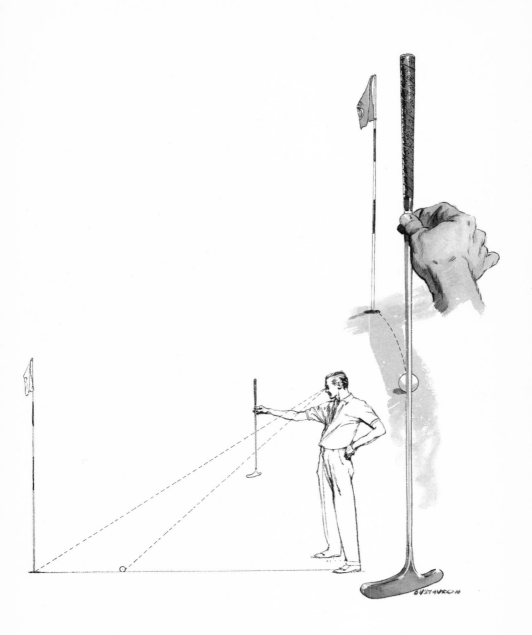

9. BILLY CASPER – WHAT MAKES A GREAT PUTTER?

By Robert Joseph Allen

"There is only one way I can show you how I handle golf shots, especially putting," Billy Casper said to me, "and that is for you to come along with me tomorrow while I play a practice round of 18 holes. Then I'll explain each shot or putt as I go."

Billy picked me up the next morning when the sun was well over the yard arm. A writer, or anyone else for that matter, rarely has an opportunity to spend an entire 18 holes all alone with a champion golfer of Billy's caliber while he explains in detail every shot he makes.

During the day Bill was as good as his word when it came to explaining not only how he did each shot, but also what his thoughts were as he approached various situations. In other words, instead of thinking to himself what he was going to do, he thought aloud for my benefit.

I will confine myself here to describing his putting, giving some of his own comments in connection with it, some of the many anecdotes he told me that had to do with his own putting, as well as the putting of others with whom he has played.

"It was a putt," Billy told me, "that gave me about the greatest thrill I have ever known in golf. It occurred during the New Orleans Open in 1958, which wound up in a play-off between Ken Venturi and myself. We had tied for the title at 278. Because the tournament had been delayed for days by torrential rains, there wasn't time to make it an 18-hole playoff. The officials decided to turn it into a sudden-death affair. Well, we both parred the first hole, which was a par-four. The second hole was a par-five, and we both hit real good drives. But on our second shots, Venturi hit into a trap while I hit on to the green about 30 feet from the pin. Ken hit a beauty of a shot from the trap and his ball came to rest less than one and a half feet from the cup—an almost sure birdie.

"I had to do at least as well in order to tie him, and that isn't easy when you are 30 feet from the hole. To go for the eagle was tempting, but as I lined up the path that my putt should take, a deep-down instinct began nagging me: *Play it safe, play it safe—just lag it up there close enough to the hole where you will have an easy putt. Don't go for it! If you do you're liable to knock it so far past you'll never get it in in only one more putt, and there will go first-prize money as well as the honor of winning this tournament.*

"Then another little voice from somewhere inside of me spoke up and said, *You know, you big lunkhead, that the only heart-breaks you've ever had in connection with putting were when you babied them and came too short—sometimes a fraction of an inch more would have dropped it in the hole. Knock it up there firmly; you might as well be hung for a lion as a sheep.*

"This last little voice appealed to me much more than the first one did, as indeed it always has throughout my lifetime, and so I stepped up and gave that ball a good bang. It rolled right up that slope and right into the cup with a firm plop, and Guy Lombardo can talk as much as he wants about the 'sweetest sounds this side of heaven,' but I want to tell you, when you are in a sudden-death playoff, the plop of the winning putt—if it's yours—well, to me that is the sweetest sound this side of heaven that I know."

More than once as I stood on one or another of the 18 greens, I thought of the phrase about Billy by pro George Ruffin. "Casper's putting touch," he said, "has the sensitivity of a safe cracker and the feel of a musician."

I asked Billy to describe to me as best he could what he felt this touch consisted of; in other words, what were the things about it of which he was conscious.

"The main thing I try to do in regard to the actual stroke itself," he said, "is a little different from what most putters try to do. I try to make my wrists act as more of a hinge at all points of the putting stroke than most anyone else I know. I do this so that the putter is moving freely, mostly by wrist motion, up from the ball, and back down through it. I try to make the blade strike the ball at the exact instant at which the blade is even with my hands, making as near as possible a vertical line from the blade up past my hands and on into my arms, with the blade passing freely forward after the ball is struck. This guards against the slight tendency I have to pull or push my putts. I try to confine the feel of the putter in my hand, as I go through the stroke, to the right thumb and index finger, or in other

135

words," he said with a smile, "that 'safe cracker's and musician's feel' that you mentioned. Doug Ford tells me that he cultivates the same light touch with his fingers by practicing the delicate stroke needed for billiards."

As the day went on I noticed an amazing thing about Billy's putting, which was that he was easily sinking more long putts—putts more than ten feet in distance—than anyone I had ever watched. To check this impression I asked him how it compared with his usual performance in a tournament. "The aggravating thing about my putting to some of my opponents," he said with a grin, "is my long putts. I've never kept track exactly, but it seems to me that I have had more long one-putt greens than short ones."

As an illustration of how much Casper's putting means to his game, take the time he won the United States Open at Winged Foot in 1959. During the 72 holes of that tournament, he three-putted only once. He one-putted 31 greens!

Of the two predominating types of putters, the great majority are those who take the putter back low to the ground on a straight line, using their wrists and arms very little, if at all—the "strokers," in a word. The people who "tap" the ball, mostly with their wrists, comprise the group to which Casper belongs. He claims the "wrist style" gives him a better sense of touch and feel, especially on fast greens. On dry, fast greens he says he tries for a more flowing stroke than if the greens are slow. However, while studying his style that day I noted that he had a tendency to tap the short putts sharply, while on the long ones I thought he "stroked" the ball much more than he seemed to think he did.

Undoubtedly one of the reasons Casper is noted for his putting is the dispatch with which he goes about it. He neglects none of the usual formalities, such as checking the path his ball must take to travel to the cup, removing any loose obstructions thereon, and calculating the distance. However, he does these things in a rapid but smooth sequence and, having completed them, he steps up and without displaying any of the usual hesitant nervousness that many pros display in connection with a long putt, but with a confident air instead, he taps his ball.

The minimum of delay which Billy uses to get his putt on the way is not by any means the fastest in the business. Doug Ford seems to have that distinction sewed up. "I putt better when I do it fast, even though I take more time with my putts than I do any other shot," Doug says. "I can see the grain and break in one look. The more I look at a putt the more lines

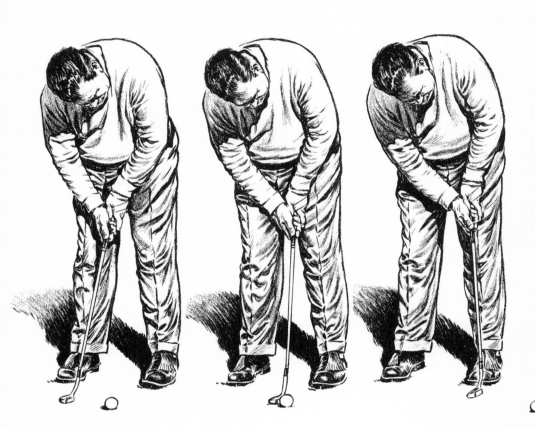

"I try," says Casper, "to make my wrists act as more of a hinge at all points of the putting stroke. I do this so the putter can move freely, mostly by wrist motion." The putter moves freely "up from the ball, and down through it. I try to make the blade strike the ball at the exact instant the blade is even with my hands." At impact, there is "as near as possible a vertical line from the blade up past my hands and on into my arms. The blade passes freely forward after the ball is hit."

and trouble I see. Therefore, I've come to depend on experience, which tells me that the first line I see is the right one."

All during his practice round that day, as Casper putted his ball, the word *competence* kept occurring to me as I sought just the right term to describe the impression he gave. There was something inspiring, too, about his putting—his was the manner of an expert displaying the skill that qualifies him as an expert. Once he has surveyed the situation, and then bends over the ball to putt, you just *know* that the ball, if it is an exceptionally long putt, is either going into the hole or mighty close to it. It is the way you'd feel about a pianist approaching his piano, if you knew it was Artur Rubinstein.

As he discussed his putting technique with me, he seemed a far cry from the Casper that Sam Snead visualized when he once said to Casper on a putting green, "Some day you're going to realize how hard it is to make those putts. All you do now is aim and fire."

I took occasion later to ask some of the leading pros who have played with Billy what in their opinion made him one of the two best putters in professional golf today.

"He is aggressive, competent, and very sure of himself, which comes from his unusually confident personality," said Billy Maxwell.

Bob Goalby thought it was because Casper "is far, far more relaxed than other people. I myself can make plenty of putts—the longer the better—when I am loose and relaxed, like when I am on the practice tee, but Billy can do it almost every time under pressure."

Dick Mayer had just one word for Billy's putting: "Gutty."

"I've watched him putt hundreds of times during the years I have played with him in tournaments," Jack Harden, co-holder of the record for one round of golf—60—in a PGA tournament, told me. "And I am certain," he said, "that his fantastic putting ability comes from an astounding natural sense of distance."

"I haven't the faintest idea why Casper putts so well," was Art Wall's testy reply to me when I asked him why he thought Billy was a great putter. "But I will tell you this," Wall said even more testily, "I'm getting awfully tired of everybody asking me that question."

"Casper's gift is in his hands," Jim Ferree said. "He has a tremendous feel in his hands for just the right distance. He is an artist with a putter like a great portrait painter is with a brush."

"I had experience as far back as 1952 with Casper when he was still

138

playing as an amateur," Eric Monti recalled, "and he was a deadly putter even then. He praticed his putting more than almost anyone I've ever known. I suppose we all tend to practice what we're good at, but Casper actually liked to practice putting—for him it was fun."

Gene Littler agrees with Monti. Gene, who is probably Casper's oldest friend on the tour, told me that Billy practiced putting more than any other touring pro he knew. "He was noted," Gene says, "around the San Diego Country Club in Chula Vista, California, for the long hours he would spend practicing putting. Bud Holscher and I played with him on a Navy team for most of the four years Billy spent in the Navy, and, while Billy likes to let on that he doesn't practice much with other clubs besides a putter, let me tell you that he didn't become one of the world's greatest golfers by rubbing a magic lamp, or something. Billy is naturally good-natured and dislikes to be considered a grind, especially of the sourly concentrated variety, but deep down I've always found him both shrewd and purposeful, and what Billy has to do, he prepares for. He has a confident, bold stroke in putting, and while I'll admit this is attuned to his character as I know it, it can be attributed much more to the conviction his almost incessant putting practice has brought him, which is that percentage-wise that is the best way to do it."

Ed Carter, former National Tournament Director for the PGA, proved to be a fan of Casper's when we asked him why he thought Billy had the reputation for being the best putter around. "I feel that it is because of his temperament—a very marvelous one for the game of golf," Carter said. "When your temperament is good, your nerves are steady. If, for instance, Billy leaves the 18th green with a 75, why, as far as the public in the grandstand would know from his demeanor, he might've had a 65. I'll never forget the time in Las Vegas when he lost the 1958 Tournament of Champions to Stan Leonard on the last hole. Instead of winning about $20,000, he received $5,000 for second place. One of the newspaper men asked him how he felt about it, and he said: 'Well, $5,000 isn't bad, is it?' Which of course was an unexpected but wonderful answer."

Billy is one of Arnie Palmer's close friends on the tour. After Arnie had won the San Diego Open in January of this year and collected his check, he escaped from the thousands of near-hysterical fans to the sanctuary of a corner of the locker room. It was there that I found him. Now that the strain of the last few holes was over and the excitement generated by the victory and the adoration of the crowd was leaving him, Arnie was just plain tired, with that exhaustion only athletes know when the last yard has been run, the last possible inch cleared in the jump, or the last putt is in the cup.

"What's on your mind?" Arnie asked, stretching out on the bench and heaving a sigh.

"I wanted to ask you what, in your opinion, makes Billy Casper such a great putter, provided, that is, you think he is a great putter."

"Oh, I think he is a great putter all right—the greatest," said Arnie. "It is a subject I've given a great deal of thought to, believe me. I would like to knock in as many putts as Billy does, but even more than that I would like to be able to *act* like he does when he's doing it—with that air of unconcern as to whether the putt drops or not. And you can bet your bottom dollar that Casper is never *too* concerned. He is a guy that just naturally won't let anything bother him too much; he feels that as long as his wife loves him and his children are crazy about him and he's got enough to eat and he is playing golf that, well, what the heck—there just isn't any more a fellow could wish for. Casper once said to me: 'As long as I am making a good living out of golf I'm not going to worry about *how* good that living is.' "

"What do you think is the secret of Casper's extraordinary putting—is it the stroke he uses?"

"No, I don't think it is his stroke," said Arnie. "As a matter of fact I don't think too much of his stroke; he takes his putter back in rather an unusual way; he lifts it up with his wrists on the back stroke, and then when he starts down he just reverses this procedure, and instead of stroking smoothly through the ball, he hits the ball something like a small boy kicking at a tin can. I don't know as that describes it very well, and I don't know of anybody else who does it just his way, but there it is—he is the greatest."

Mrs. Casper agreed with Arnie that her husband is not one to mix up the proper order of the important things of life. "When he has a poor round he never takes it out on his family," she says. "Whenever he has a real bad day—and who doesn't?—he comes home, perhaps a little quieter than usual, and will watch television for a while because it seems to sorta act on his mind like an eraser on a blackboard. In an hour or so he is as chipper as ever."

His most outstanding trait of character, in her estimation, is his capacity for being "level-headed."

140

While we were playing that practice round, I asked Casper about what Arnie had said concerning his sharply tapping his putts instead of using a smoothly flowing stroke. "Yes, it's true I prefer to tap the ball rather than stroke the ball while putting," he said. He also told me he tried to hit the ball just hard enough to get it past the cup in the event it didn't drop in. But as for uphill putts that were off-line, he always hoped the putt would stop below the cup if the green slanted towards him. "I think," he said, "it's safe to say that 99 out of 100 golfers can make a short uphill putt with more certainty than they can a downhill putt.

"One thing," he went on to say, "every beginning golfer should keep in the forefront of his mind is that 40 to 50 per cent of his strokes must be made with the putter. Ben Hogan also had some ideas about putting which he expressed very well when he said: 'I have always contended golf is one game and putting is another. One game is played in the air, the other is played on the ground.'

"There certainly is a lot of psychology gets into putting," Casper told me at another point. "Take Bobby Locke's hickory-shafted, rusty, dilapidated old putter for instance. I read where he said it is about 45 years old. Perhaps this is the reason he loves it so well, but one thing is certain: in his hands it is a magic wand that wafts golf balls into the cup and made him, during the time he was playing in tournaments regularly, probably the best putter in the world. He won five national opens with it that I know of: British, South African, Egyptian, French, and Mexican, and a raft of tournaments in this country, Britain, and elsewhere.

"Then there is a medical doctor, by the name of Mark J. Bach, who believes that the biggest influence on putting is exercised by a remarkable mechanism in the inner ear, the part of the body that lets us keep our balance, as the saying goes. He says that when it gets out of kilter, we have the feeling known as dizziness. It is his contention, as I understand him, that when a golfer known for his good putting has a bad day, that it is caused by this doohickey in the ear getting slightly out of whack."

Mike Souchak has a system he uses when putting, though it is not unique with him, of picking a spot on the green that is about a foot from the ball and directly in line with the cup. Then he concentrates on hitting the ball over this spot and on towards the cup, something like the way the front and rear sights of a gun are utilized when aimed at a target."

Casper uses the reverse-overlap grip and stands more erect than usual, with his feet about 14 inches apart, playing the ball inside his left heel

141

and approximately four-and-a-half inches in front of his left toe. He explains that he prefers the reverse-overlap grip because it creates the feeling in his hands that they move as one during the stroke.

"My apparent relaxation when I'm putting is not as unassumed as it might seem to some people," he assured me. "I make a practice of keeping my grip easy but firm, and my weight divided so both feet carry an equal share of the burden, and quite a bit of weight it is too," he said in a good-natured jibe at the extra avoirdupois he carries around with him.

No one should get the idea, however, that Casper is what is known as fat. He couldn't have won all the golf tournaments he has, including the National Open, beating all the best players in the world on any given set of four days, without having a very fine, well-coordinated physique. Any close examination of Casper's physical condition reveals to the observing eye that he does have some extra weight undoubtedly, but it is very firmly distributed. To the knowing eye he gives an impression of tremendous strength, an impression that is heightened by the fact that he is light on his feet.

He claims the most important thing to concentrate on while putting is speed—not the line, as so many weekend golfers seem to think. He told me that he rarely if ever thinks of the line after he finishes lining up the putt and settles himself over the ball. From that point on he thinks only of the desired speed, or force, of the blow necessary to carry it to the hole. He keeps his hands in front of his left leg, somewhat ahead of the ball because he can give the ball overspin in this way, which makes it run smoothly and tightly along the green on the way to the cup, the way a well-thrown bowling ball does as it streaks down the alley towards the pins.

The Casper sense of humor is never-failing, as was evidenced by his treatment of a story that gained wide credence a year or so ago to the effect that he was not immune to some of the omnipresent superstitions cherished by leading golfers, and had, after missing a few putts, deserted the mallet-type putter with which he won the United States Open; not a temporary desertion either—he had, they said, given it away! When Casper was taxed with this, he would explain that this putter got so much publicity after the extraordinary performance it gave in one-putting those 31 greens for him during the Open that it acquired a star complex and began showing temperament at times when he was most dependent on it.

(Actually, at the urging of the United States Golf Association, he presented the putter to Golf House in New York City, where it is now part of a permanent exhibit of golf memorabilia.)

But when asked by the more gullible why he didn't keep the putter out of pure sentiment anyway, even if provoked with it at the moment, he would laugh and say: "I guess I'm just the cruel type."

ACCURATE APPROACH PUTTING

By Skee Riegel

Villanova, Pennsylvania

The two best approach putters I have ever seen are Bobby Locke and Jack Burke, Jr. It is absolutely uncanny the way they can be standing 30 feet or more from the hole on almost any given occasion and then lob the ball to within a foot or so of the cup. Surprisingly, neither one gives hardly any consideration to the line when approach putting. They concentrate almost wholly on the distance. Because, through a feeling of distance, the line comes automatically. But you can't figure this distance out in your head. You simply have to feel it by leaving the judgment entirely up to your eye. *Look at the situation this way: Most long putts are missed by being way short of the cup or way past it, not because they were way off line. Few persons are so utterly without a sense of direction that they will stroke a putt four or more feet off line.* Yet, by failing to concentrate on the distance, they very often leave a putt six or more feet short or beyond the cup.

THE RIGHT WAY TO PUTT

By Byron Nelson

Roanoke, Texas

I maintain that putting is one of the most controversial points in the game of golf. But regardless of this, each player is trying to achieve the same ultimate goal and the putter is the only club in the bag which allows the player so wide a choice of grip, stance and action. However, there are basic principles that must still be followed. *First, hold the putter firmly with the left hand, but not tightly enough to restrict the movement. Stroke the ball with the right hand. In other words, the left hand guides and the right hand provides the power.* Too much of either will make you pick up the clubhead and this makes you push or cut across the ball. Good putters keep their feet close together for balance and they play the ball off the big toe of the left foot. If the ball is played too far back it will be cut because you will hit down on it. If it is played too far forward you will hit up on the ball, imparting topspin. A good putter stands directly over the ball and keeps his head and shoulders perfectly still. He should keep the club low going back and low going through the ball.

GROOVED PUTTING STROKE

By Smiley Quick

Pomona, California

One of the most important assets in golf is a grooved, repeating putting stroke. It's a lot harder to achieve this than one might think. I did it with the aid of a small mitre box about 15 inches long. This is a plywood box with a felt-lined bottom and no ends. The walls are about four inches high. The walls are parallel and are about one inch from the heel and toe of the putter blade. *The box is so narrow it will keep your putter on line and prevent you from cutting across the ball.* This box won't help with regard to how hard to hit putts but it sure will give you a grooved stroke if you work at trying to develop one. To build a mitre box, I recommend using plywood one-eighth of an inch thick for the bottom and about one-quarter of an inch thick for the sides. The reason I like a thin bottom is that there's very little drop between the end of the mitre box and the green. This makes for a smoother roll and gives you a better idea how you're stroking the ball. P.S. Be sure your walls are absolutely parallel. Build a crooked box and you're in trouble.

MAKING PUTTS FIND THE HOLE

By Sam Snead

White Sulphur Springs, West Virginia

Any pro will tell you that more putts are missed by being mishit than by being misjudged. You can line up a putt all you want, but it won't possibly travel along that line unless it is struck precisely in the way your putting touch has told you it should be struck. Mechanically, the soundest way to contact the ball with your putter is in such a way that the face of the putter applies overspin to the ball. With overspin, the ball will tend to roll over indentations, tiny pebbles, and other obstacles that would ordinarily throw a spinning ball off line. Spin is usually applied to a putt when the putter is lifted high off the ground on the backswing. Thus, you have to hit down on the ball during the downswing, a stroke which makes the ball skid along the green rather than roll over it. *To avoid hitting down on my putts and thus spinning them off line, I take the putter back as low to the ground as possible without actually touching it.* In this way, I am able to bring the face of my putter back to the ball squarely and in such a way that it never strikes the ball above its perimeter.

10. HORTON SMITH DISCUSSES PRACTICAL PUTTING

With Joan Flynn Dreyspool

"I started putting on sand greens in my home town, Springfield, Missouri, and I've always felt that helped me most in my study of putting," observes Horton Smith, considered by many to be the best putter golf has produced in the last 35 years.

"The sand was rather loose, not firm like the original clay-based sand greens at Pinehurst. The ball left a track, a tracer, a visual impression of the line. To experiment, I hit the ball every which way; off the left foot, right foot and middle. I stood close, away, upright, bent over. I used different grips, different motions. If I hit too much downwards, I could see where the blade of my club dug up some sand. If I happened to flip the ball with my blade, I could see the skip marks.

"I didn't need any crystal ball to convince myself that if the hole was there and the track of the ball was going away from it, the margin for error was within the position of my putter's face when it contacted the ball.

"Inevitably I came back to the basic principle of the square blade, the right angle or T-square position. Call it what you will. My general pattern for putting is a clear picture of alignment—right hand parallel with putter face; palm of the right hand facing toward the line throughout the stroke. Keep it square. Keep it straight back or inside the line. Keep it low. Keep it smooth."

Square. Straight. Smooth. The words that embody Horton Smith's putting philosophy might aptly describe his way of life. In 1926 at the age of 18, Horton Smith turned professional. Three years later, the "Joplin Ghost" blazed his way to golfing glory by winning seven tournaments, clinching runner-up spots in four others and emerging as 1929's leading money winner with $14,000 plus, a lot of money in those days. At 21 he was the youngest golfer ever to play on a Ryder Cup team. He won the first Masters Tournament in 1934 at 26, and two years later he won it again.

Today, following his most recent victory over Hodgkin's disease, Horton Smith, soft-spoken, well groomed, vibrant in his 53rd year, is still enough of a perfectionist at golf to apologize for a 78 he shot the day before. "I had an eight on the 15th hole," said Horton, who is pro at the Detroit Golf Club. "I tried too fancy a shot and went in the water."

Savoring the subject of putting for dessert, Horton Smith discussed other aspects of the game first. "I believe there is a pattern for golf," he began. "Good posture is fundamental; good balance and a general sense of freedom throughout the swing with a positive release of the right-arm action. The stance should be wide enough to base or balance the swing required, without restricting the body movement and live hand action. The grip requires a finger-and-palm hold in the left hand, with the left hand over enough to the right to strengthen the hand and firm up the left arm and shoulder muscle. The right hand is a finger grip with the palm facing the target. Elbows down and in toward the player's body. I believe in left side leadership and a connected swing which means all parts move in harmony, a fluid action. It always reminds me of that song, 'The foot bone's connected to the ankle bone, the ankle bone's connected to the shin bone, the shin bone's connected to the knee bone' and so on up through the thigh, hip, waist, shoulder, arms, hands.

"That should be the pattern of the swing, generally inside, or inside-out or inside-straight-through, but always with live hands and body support and assistance. The poor player disconnects his swing sometimes as soon as six inches back of the ball. Unfortunately, a lot of people stand to a ball with no idea where they are going. This falls under the heading of alignment, and alignment is a must, whether it's a drive, a putt or any other shot. Unfortunately, too, so many people have no idea of how much of a swing they need to get to where they want to be.

"The golfer must educate himself to the point where he can look at his target and say, 'I think this is a 75-yard shot, so I'll take my nine-iron (or whatever he needs) and play a three-quarter shot.' There's nothing I would like better than to have a golf course marked off like a gridiron for yardage, but of course, golf courses aren't, so I try to line off each shot mentally, zone it and key it to my own swing, whether I need a full swing, a three-quarter swing, a half swing or quarter swing. I think of a full swing as one with the hands about shoulder high; the three-quarter as chest high; the half as hip high and the quarter as knee high.

"If you practice the knee-high, hip-high, chest-high, shoulder-high patterns and study the distances you can reach with each swing and club, you begin to associate a certain degree of swing for a required distance.

"Superior players, great players, accomplish this by skill or instinct, the result of practice, and a keen sense of distance, feel, sight, position and general relationship of himself, the ball and shot required.

"The less gifted or experienced golfer has to acquire this through discipline and practice and an honest self-appraisal of his own abilities. Once he has made up his mind as to the distance and degree of swing required and has selected the club he thinks is right, then he should hit the shot with complete confidence in himself. Chances are, he'll be right more often than not.

"Indecision is costly, whether it's a putt, pitch or pivot, but the real finesse in a golf swing is to know how to cut down or build up power and the swing and adapt both to the particular shot.

"Sometimes when I teach a beginner, I have him or her grip the club at the bottom of the leather; heels no more than two or three inches apart. Then I have him swing about knee high. The swing is a miniature of everything, a requisite for reduced power. In this position for a short shot, there is no way anyone can knock the ball clear over the green unless he completely tops it.

"For practice and practical purposes, this swing can be built up; slightly wider stance and stronger swing for hip high; then chest high and on through to the full or shoulder-high swing.

"One thing I am convinced of—to play good golf, you have to have free action, a free right hand and arm, whether you're putting, driving or taking any other shot. You can't have free expression of your right hand or arm if you don't to some degree cock the right elbow and/or right wrist. It's all a pattern—basic principles discovered through trial and error. And this is especially true on the putting green."

"Years ago," he recalled, "there wasn't the concentration or emphasis on putting technique or knowledge there is now. Putting was almost belittled, a necessary evil to finish out the hole. The more I played, the more I recognized and accepted the importance of putting. As a kid, I was fairly slight and didn't hit the ball very far, so through necessity I decided I would have to make up shots on the green.

"Putting now is the most decisive part of the game, but you certainly

can't win unless you have a fine game otherwise. The fellow who is hitting the ball far and straight and hitting the greens is going to capitalize on his putting more.

"Snead has missed a number of important crucial putts which has given his putting bad advertising, but he's certainly been a good putter. Television has shown how good he is. Doug Ford is unquestionably a fine putter; also Casper. So is Jerry Barber. Arnold Palmer is a beautiful putter. I like his technique, a firm left and definite hit with the right. I wouldn't be surprised if Palmer were the greatest golfer of all time. He starts out with a fine attitude, a fine mental and physical balance. He's quite well-adjusted; he has a good fighting spirit with enough self-discipline and control that never gets seriously out of hand. He can burn and fume with a bad shot just like anybody else, but he doesn't dwell on it. He forgets it and resolves to use that energy on the next shot. He has a fine mechanical game, power—unusual power—and I feel, a very fine putting technique.

"Consider what has happened to Ben Hogan's putting," Horton Smith said. "His taking a long time over his putts is nothing new. He possibly takes a little more time now, but when he was a good putter, he still stood a long time, apparently motionless with his putter behind the ball, longer than any good putter I have ever seen. I don't think Ben can operate that technique now. He's older and his nerves have changed a little bit—it happens to us all.

"In putting as in any aspect of the game, *it's easier to continue a motion than it is to originate one*. Therefore, I feel the solution to Hogan's problem might be to take as long as he wants getting set, but once he places the putter in back of the ball—his final check—then he should immediately take the putter back and continue his stroke through to the hole. This continuous motion will relieve the tension and offer more fluidity.

"Everyone on the circuits nowadays is a good putter. If he isn't, he doesn't stand a chance. To me, the ideal way of evaluating a round of golf is not only by score, but by how many greens were hit in par figures, plus the total of putts and the total footage of the putts sunk.

"The fewest putts I ever had were 17 once in Springfield, Missouri," he recalled, "but you can't strike an average on the putts. It depends upon the size of the green and conditions. I think the best round I ever had was the one at the Masters in Augusta in 1934. I had 26 putts, but my total footage was about 65 feet. What actually happened, I chipped some up close off the edge of the green to within six inches of the cup; a couple

156

of other times I had one-footers. However, this was not a fine putting round. It was a fine chipping and placement round, but the putts I sunk were decisive. On the 71st hole, I dropped a 15-footer for a birdie to go in front of Craig Wood by a shot, and on the final hole, I holed a very treacherous putt of about two-and-a-half feet for a par to win by that shot. The wind was blowing very hard and it was a very fast, slippery, tricky putt. It played to the left edge of the hole with at least a two-inch borrow.

"Dick Metz, Jimmy Hines and I once played in a specialist tournament at the Cavalier Course in Virginia Beach. I was doing the chipping and putting. I sunk 180 feet of putts. That's an average of ten feet per hole, but of course, the result was I holed three long ones and wasn't chipping as close to the pin as I should have.

"I had 23 putts in the final round of the St. Paul Open in 1941, when I shot 63 and won by one shot. I holed a 20-footer on the final hole for an eagle three on a short par-five.

"I've never had too many really critically missed putts. On the 36th green at the Miami Biltmore in the mid-Thirties, during a four-ball tournament, I missed a two-foot putt which caused Paul Runyan and me to lose to Dick Metz and Ky Laffoon. I missed a two-foot putt on the 71st green at Glen Falls in 1938 to drop into a tie with Denny Shute; then I lost in the play-off."

Fred Corcoran used to introduce Horton Smith at banquets during the Democrats' long reign in the Thirties and Forties as "the only man who hasn't three-putted a green since the Republican Administration."

"Horton never putted with his glove on," Corcoran, now tournament head of the International Golf Association, reported recently. "He never wanted to shake hands during a tournament, either. You'd be surprised how many of the pros don't want to. People unknowingly crush your fingers and a pro has to go out of his way to protect his hands."

"Throughout the years, no matter how many experiments I made, I always came back to the basic principle of the square blade," Horton Smith reflected. "The left hand holds and steadies the putter and guides the stroke, but the right hand supplies the feel, the action and the hit. I believe the right wrist should break, and I try to oppose any break of the left.

"I use the reverse-overlap grip, with the left index finger over the little finger of the right hand. Both thumbs are placed squarely on the shaft. The left hand grips with both palm and fingers, conducive to the firmness required, but the right hand holds the club in the fingers, contributing to the freedom and action necessary for a right-hand hit. My stance, like everything else about the putt, is square; eyes directly over the ball; body in close, without crowding. The main thing I am after is right-hand action without body movement.

"Just as a pitch or short shot is a miniature of the full swing, a short putt is even more of a miniature compared with a long putt. If you were to flick a ball underhanded for a distance of two feet, you would find no noticeable movement in your body. All you need is to flip the right hand. Yet if you were to try to flick that ball ten, 20, 30, 40 or 50 feet, for each added distance, there must be more action with the right hand and forearm.

"Conduct your own experiment. Take a golf ball on a carpet or practice green. Without using a putter, but using your right hand only, try to direct that ball to your target. First of all, when you're standing up, you find you can't roll that ball; you have to pitch it. Immediately your body has to lower itself closer to the ground. So now, bend over and pretend the palm of the right hand is the clubface of the putter. Try to send the ball in a straight line, two feet, four feet, six feet and so on. Instinctively that right hand, when it gets the message from your brain, is stronger, more active, for the added distance.

"The clubface of your putter is the palm of your right hand. The putter is the shortest club in the bag. Why? Because putting is the most miniature shot in golf, the most precise, the most demanding; so all extraneous motion and height must be removed. The moment you call upon other parts of your body to contribute to this search for accuracy, you're widening your margin for error. You don't have the width of a fairway here to cover your mistakes. You have a cup no wider than four-and-a-quarter inches.

"Precision is your premise! Indecision is your foe!

"The perfect combination is the wedding of stance, alignment and technique—all physical—with the mental, a sense of distance and tempo plus your navigation or reading of the green. The physical can be taught directly; but the mental you have to learn indirectly—by trial and error, practice, experiment, instinct, feel.

"How many times have you stood over a putt and said, 'I'm going to miss this one.' You might as well add an extra stroke to your score right there.

158

" 'You have to turn a negative thought into a positive one,' I tell my pupils. This is true on any shot, especially with putting. Trust yourself, then stroke the putt. One of the reasons people thought I was a good putter was that I never complained of it. If I didn't make a putt, there was a reason for it. I would ask myself: Did I keep the blade square? Did I read it right? Was I firm enough? Was I decisive?

"If the answer was 'no' to any of these, the putt deserved to be missed."

THE LEFT-HAND GUIDE

By Art Wall, Jr.

Pocono Manor, Pennsylvania

For me, the distance of a putt has always been a bigger problem than the line of it. Two years ago, Jack Burke gave me a suggestion that has helped me considerably, however. On putts 15 feet or longer, he advised me to visualize the putt as being half the actual distance, take a practice stroke at what I would judge to be that distance, and then hit the actual putt twice as hard as I had practiced. While this method may seem to be the long way round, it has nevertheless proved to be a surer method of judging distance. Once you have the distance problem conquered, putting then becomes entirely a matter of keeping the ball on the line you have seen. To do this, I take the putter straight back, employing little or no wrist break, unless, of course, the putt is rather long. *In making the downstroke, I let the left hand dominate. Let me put it this way: I lead with the left but stroke with the right.* In following through, I try to keep the back of my left hand traveling directly at the back of the hole. In this manner, I eliminate the disastrous tendency most people have of flipping the head of the putter with the right hand.

160

THE RELAXED PUTTER

By Walter Hagen

Traverse City, Michigan

There isn't a golfer alive who hasn't felt the pressure of a match while putting. Despite my reputation as a pressure putter, I often felt tension creeping into my stroke. Although neither I (nor anyone else) ever completely conquered this feeling of pressure, I did learn to cope with it. As we all well know, the putting stroke is the most easily affected shot in golf. After a few jerked putts, your confidence goes. And then your whole game comes apart at the seams. My problem, then, was to learn how to loosen up after I had jerked a putt or two. To accomplish this, I used a simple little trick which anybody can use. *I placed a golf ball between the shaft and the last two fingers of my left hand, thus placing the pressure of that hand more in the fingers, with which you are less apt to jerk a putt than with the palm of the hand.* Try this little gimmick a few times, and I'm sure you will be surprised at how quickly it loosens up your stroke, how much more easily you can return to your natural, free stroke.

THE PUTTING STROKE

By Gene Sarazen

Germantown, New York

Putting is a very individual thing. Therefore, the most important thing you can do is to get yourself set comfortably. Mechanically speaking, there are really only two points you have to be sure of. Your left elbow should be pointed toward the target and your right elbow should be braced against your right side. However you set your feet or wherever you position the ball is entirely up to you. It is worth keeping in mind, however, that the greatest putters are those who use short, compact backswings, as does Walter Hagen. *I have found it helpful in checking the length of my backswing to place my right forefinger straight down the shaft.* In addition to making my backswing compact, this habit enables me to maintain the clubface square to the hole. Again I say—as with all other shots—be sure not to break your wrists.

THE TAP PUTT

By Bob Rosburg

Napa, California

In taking the putter back, I hood the clubface by breaking the left hand underneath. *By this I mean, I turn my left hand counterclockwise as I take the putter back.* Then, as I come down with the putter, my left hand moves clockwise so that the face of the putter is square to the ball at impact. This hooding and un-hooding action, which might be termed a sort of reverse pronation, gives me more solid contact with the ball—a very firm tap. If I don't putt in this manner, I find that my right hand sometimes dominates on the downstroke and that I hit the ball with the face of the putter slightly closed. With this tap technique, I concentrate a good deal more on distance than direction, as do most tournament players. I make certain I give the ball a good, solid crack with the putter, and I make sure I take a short enough backswing to do so. Odd as it may seem, I never think about taking the putter back square to the ball. On a putt that breaks left to right, I take the putter back a bit outside the intended line of roll. I do just the reverse on a putt that will break from right to left; that is, I take the putter back inside the line of roll.

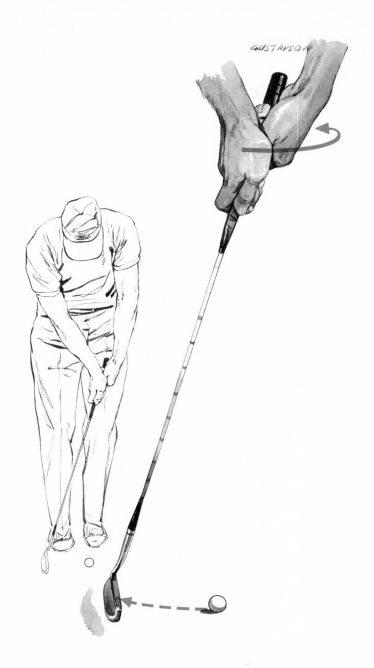

THE KEY TO ACCURATE PUTTING

By George Low

Tap City, California

In taking the putter back, break the left wrist first. This causes the putter to be taken back inside. Your weight should be mainly on the left foot, and most of the action should come from the elbows down. Don't move the body. Always remember to take a firm hold on the putter, with both thumbs on top of the shaft. In my book the thumb is the most sensitive finger. When you reach into your pocket for a coin, for example, the last finger to touch the coin is your thumb. And, of course, the thumb plays a vital role when you pull the coin out. That's why placing the thumbs on top of the shaft can help your putting stroke considerably. With the thumbs properly positioned, it is easier to develop a simple, consistent putting stroke. *I have found it easier to contact the ball with the center of the putter if the ball is addressed off the heel of the blade and the left wrist breaks immediately, forcing the putter to be taken back on the inside. This means, of course, that the putter is brought to the ball from the inside, along the same line followed when it was taken back.* Many players who take the putter straight back from the ball are prone to cut across the ball from the outside in on the downstroke. This can be avoided if the left wrist breaks at the start of the backstroke.

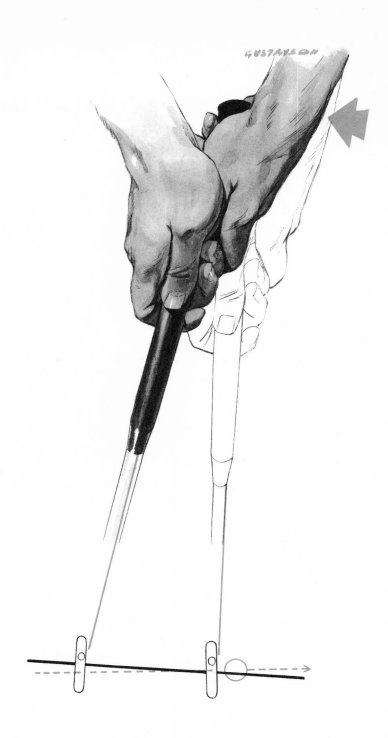

ADVANTAGES OF THE LAG PUTT

By Bobby Jones

Atlanta, Georgia

"Never up, never in" is a proposition that has never made sense to me. Of course, we never know but that the ball which is on line and stops short would have holed out. But we do know that the ball that ran past did not hole out. *It seems to me much more expedient always to try to gauge the strength of a putt so that the ball, if it does not go in, will stop on line with the hole or just past it. Then you will have four sides of the hole instead of the target of scarcely an inch which is available to the man who bangs for the back of the cup.* When you have a curling putt across a slope, therefore, try to drop the ball slowly into the upper side of the hole, making certain of borrowing at least enough from the slope. If you make the mistake on the other side, the consequence will be more serious, for every turn of the ball will take it farther from the hole. One thing more while on the subject of putting: the idea promulgated by some that any sort of putter or putting stroke can impart an overspin to the ball which will cause it to duck into the hole is sheer trash. A ball rolling across the putting surface has no spin which will affect its travel, nor can any side spin endure after the ball settles down for a roll.

PERCENTAGE PUTTING

By Fred Haas, Jr.

New Orleans, Louisiana

Most golfers miss putts on the low or "amateur" side for the simple reason that they don't know how to play the breaks on the greens. For over a year now, I've been using a putting system that has saved me many important strokes. If I had used this system since turning professional in 1946, I might be some $100,000 richer today. In a nutshell, here's the idea. *On left-breaking putts, I line up and hit the ball on the toe of the putter. On putts breaking right, I hit the ball on the heel of the putter. And, with straight putts, I hit the ball dead-center.* Hitting the ball on the heel will start it out to the left, thus helping on putts that break to the right. The opposite naturally holds true for the putt breaking left. This system is not too effective on long putts, but it's very helpful from within six feet of the cup where many strokes can be saved with effective putting. *By lining up and hitting putts this way, you can eliminate a one-third chance of error.* Any putt, if hit at the right speed, can go in only three directions, left, center, and right. If a putt breaks to the left, you must avoid heeling the ball. However, if you play it off the toe of the putter, the chance of heeling it becomes nearly impossible if the basic stroke is smooth. By doing this you have practically eliminated the chance for the ball to go to the left of the hole. In other words, you've got the percentages working for you.

11. VERY IMPORTANT PUTTERS

By Carlos Bohlin

The best putter at the country club is Dimmy, who picked up much of what he knows about putting by misspending his youth in pool halls. He uses a toy of a club that looks as though it had come in a box of Crackerjack, and he breaks every rule in the book by hitting down on the ball with no perceptible follow-through.

But it goes in the hole.

Betty is the best putter over at Kenwood. She uses a mallet-head of indeterminate vintage, and she hits up on the ball with a long, sweeping follow-through. It too goes in the hole.

Then there is that guy at Springdale who is built like a truck-driver and has the touch of a hairdresser; the old gent at Elmwood who putts with his shoulders; and that screwball at Fair Acres who putts between his legs.

But all of them have one thing in common. They can putt the eyes out of a squirrel.

The more you investigate the mystery of putting the clearer it becomes to you that no one has ever really satisfactorily solved it. Everybody knows how to putt; that is, at some time or another they can do it. But nobody really knows how to putt; that is, they don't really know how they do it.

As a matter of plain fact, they can't even make up their minds what type of club is best to use. Putters—the clubs, that is—are as individual as neckties. At most pro shops today, you get just as wide a choice. On the market there are literally dozens of types of putters, each as distinctly different to the eye as a polka dot is from a red stripe. At one time you were blissfully limited to a choice of, say, five—Calamity Jane, Mills, Blue Goose, Schenectady, Cash-in—but today the choice is maddeningly wider, although most of them are but subtle variations on these original five.

To show how individualistic putting can be, let's examine the pet theories of some of the greatest putters who ever lived: Walter Travis, Jerry Travers, Walter Hagen, Bob Jones, Horton Smith, Paul Runyan, and Bobby Locke. Each of these men played winning championship golf, and their success at it was largely due to their ability to get the ball in the hole with a putter.

Of the six, Walter J. Travis was the oldest, the oddest, and perhaps the best putter of the bunch. A transplanted Australian who lived on Long Island, Travis never hit a golf shot until he was 35 years old. Less than two years later, he became proficient enough to reach the semi-finals of the National Amateur. Two years after that, he won it.

Bearded and stern, he looked a little like one of the Smith Brothers. Travis learned practically everything he knew about the game by studying golf books religiously and then tirelessly experimenting on the practice tee with what he had read, accepting or rejecting whatever he thought was sound or unsound for his limited physical means. In the process, he became phenomenally adept with the putter.

By 1904, when Travis was 43, he had won three of the last four Amateur Championships. He decided to try his hand at the British Amateur, a title no one from foreign soil had ever won. In an effort to shake himself out of a surprising putting slump, he borrowed a Schenectady putter from a friend on the day before the championship began at Sandwich. This was a putter with the shaft inserted in the center of a mallet-head, and was so named because a Mr. A. W. Knight of that city had been the first to use it.

In the final, which Travis managed to reach despite an unsympathetic gallery and a cross-eyed caddie, he beat Ted Blackwell, the longest hitter in British golf at the time. Although Blackwell frequently outdrove him by 60 yards or more, Travis won the match and the championship, 4 and 3, by sinking 30- and 40-footers with the abandon of a man knocking in two-footers for a nickel Nassau. So incredible did Travis's victory seem that the British barred Schenectady putters for more than 40 years.

Not uncharacteristically, Travis won his last major tournament, the Metropolitan Amateur, in New York, at the age of 50 by canning a 30-footer on the last green in the finals.

Travis employed a reverse overlap grip with his putter. This is to say, the first finger of his left hand overrode the little finger of his right. Delicately, yet firmly, he grasped the club first with his right hand, with the thumb straight down the shaft, and then he placed the left thumb on the shaft and in the palm of the right hand.

The actual stroke was initiated by the left wrist, he claimed, although the putt itself was a job that was soon taken over by the right hand. To be more particular, he felt that the chief instrument in the stroke should be the right forefinger. At all times the body was absolutely motionless, all movement being confined to the wrists.

In starting his backstroke, Travis liked to keep the clubhead as close to the ground as possible. For the first two or three inches, he took it straight back from the ball, then he withdrew it slightly inwards, how much so being determined by the length of the putt.

As soon as the ball was struck, Travis relaxed his grip with the left hand. The right hand then took over, permitting the clubhead to travel as long as possible on a straight line toward the hole.

Travis choked his putter as many as six inches. He played the ball as close to his right foot as he comfortably could. His right elbow was kept tucked against his side, his left elbow pointed on a line parallel to the hole. He believed very strongly that if you were never up you were never in.

"Solitary practice is of little use," he said. "The human element in the shape of an opponent is lacking. For this reason, I particularly recommend practicing on a competitive basis, and always for some stake, no matter how small, even though it only be a black cigar."

Jerome D. Travers had a somewhat similar name, but in many respects he was the antithesis of Walter J. Travis. While Travis played his best golf during the September of his life, Travers was winning tournaments (and sometimes trouncing Travis himself) at the age of 18. Beginning in 1907, Travers, an amateur of independent means all his life, won the first of four Amateur Championships, a record since surpassed only by Bob Jones and equalled by no one else. Two of these wins were successful defenses of his title. In 1915 he also won the National Open.

Travers was not a naturally gifted putter. But, in becoming the best match-player of his day, he made himself into a very sharp putter in an effort to counteract erratic tendencies that sometimes forced him to drive with irons on a tight course.

Like Travis, Travers preferred a Schenectady. He employed an interlocking grip, and pinched the nail of his right thumb against the shaft. He kept his palms directly in opposition and held the club mainly with the fingers. His stance was very open. The stroke, he felt, was executed with a combination of the hands, wrists, and arms. At all times, he insisted, the body should remain "absolutely immovable."

One further tip, he felt, had done much to improve his putting. He never allowed the full weight of the clubhead to rest against the green. Rather, he held it lightly, so that the bottom of the head just touched the turf.

With Travis, Francis Ouimet and Chick Evans, Travers monopolized amateur golf for many years. The last three also did more than just hold their own in open competition as well. As a matter of record, the only professional who was able to win the National Open between 1912 and 1920—no championships were held in 1917 or 1918—was Walter Hagen, who streamlined putting technique to such an extent that many of his methods and mannerisms are still being beavered today.

Hagen's preference in putters ran to blades, usually with little loft, stiff shafts and extraordinary weight. Hagen once commented that a heavy putter was easier to handle under pressure than a light one. In an effort to overcome putting slumps, he often practiced with a golf ball held against the shaft by the last two fingers of his left hand. This helped him regain the sense of touch he wanted in his forefingers. From this practice, he developed the polo grip, as it came to be called, which consisted of a curved protrusion of about an inch in length on the underside of the shaft near the top, much in the manner of the grip on a polo mallet.

In assuming his stance, Hagen set himself up square to the hole, his body facing at right angles to the intended line. This was in sharp contrast to the wide open stances that had been so popular for years. He kept his feet about as wide apart as his shoulders, with the left withdrawn approximately six inches behind his right. Most of his weight was placed on his left leg, and the ball was played just off, and slightly inside, the toe of his left shoe. The stance was inimitably his, and came to be known for many years as simply "the Hagen stance."

Hagen has the long, unmuscular hands of a concert pianist. They were the source of his golfing genius. Even today, when you chat with him, you can't help noticing how beautifully he handles them. With his sleeves rolled up just a turn, a cigarette poised fragilely between the forefinger and middle finger, he uses his hands to dramatize practically everything he says, with the result that they are in a constant state of motion, whirling and twirling about him like a couple of trained doves.

Naturally, it was Hagen's hands that took over the job of stroking his putts. When he was right, he had the sure, deft touch of a brain surgeon. He kept the blade closed on the backstroke and slightly inside the intended line. Then he would catch the fat part of the ball, sometimes so surely that he would start for the cup to pick out the ball before it had halfway rolled there.

With Hagen, the reverse overlapping grip with the putter became standard practice. Another to use it effectively was Bob Jones, who felt that proper putting was predominately a right-hand stroke. Jones kept his hands "carefully opposed," as he so carefully put it, with the wrists working "exactly" against each other.

Jones felt that putting is a game within a game, and he considered Walter Travis "the greatest putter the game has known." Unlike Travis, however, he did not believe that there should be a concentrated effort to keep the body still. Rather, he felt, it should be allowed to move so as not to break the rhythm of your stroke. He felt, furthermore, that the length of the backstroke was immaterial and should be disregarded.

Jones also disagreed with Travis that you were never in if you were never up. "Of course," he wrote during his prime, "we never know but that the ball which is on line and stops short would have holed out. But we *do* know that ball that ran past *did not* hole out."

Jones addressed the ball in a relatively upright way, facing slightly toward the hole, his heels almost touching, his toes turned outwards. His hands were positioned slightly ahead of the ball. He would then spank the ball with his right hand so that the ball "died" either in or very near to the cup.

During the early stages of his unparalleled career, Jones used a Ray-Mills type of putter. Later he switched to a Schenectady. In 1920, however, he was given an old Winton by Jim Maiden, brother of Stewart Maiden, Jones's pro and mentor at his home club of East Lake. It was rather short as putters go, slightly goose-necked, and very lofted. The wooden shaft was split slightly, necessitating three wrappings of string. Jones referred to it affectionately as Calamity Jane.

Jones won the 1923 National Open, his first major championship, with

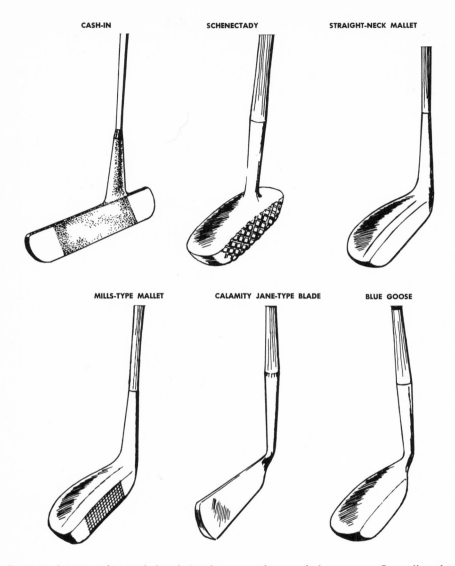

CASH-IN   **SCHENECTADY**   **STRAIGHT-NECK MALLET**

MILLS-TYPE MALLET   **CALAMITY JANE-TYPE BLADE**   **BLUE GOOSE**

Few people can make up their minds what type of putter is best to use. In reality, the choice is as individual as choosing neckties. Here are six classic types that have been popular down through the years. They are the prototypes of many of today's popular putters.

it, but constant buffing made the face irregular. Jones then had a duplicate made, which he labeled Calamity Jane II and with which he won 12 major titles. The club is on display today in a glass case at Golf House, the headquarters of the United States Golf Association, in New York City.

Horton Smith, one of the best putters to come along between the world wars, started showing his stuff in 1930, the year Jones retired from competition. Tall and angular, Smith belied an awkward appearance with one of the smoothest putting styles ever to grace the tournament trail. He used a modified Hagen stance, addressed the ball very deliberately, and swung the blade of his putter as though he were pouring molasses.

Smith was superseded as the top putter on the tour by Paul Runyan, a man many pros consider to be the strongest putter, day in and day out, of any player in modern golf.

By all odds, the best putter to have been seen in postwar golf has been Bobby Locke, of South Africa. Locke's touch was so uncanny during the few years he monopolized the circuit that he had most of the pros talking to themselves and some of them beating their heads against lockers in frustration.

"I never saw anything to equal it," says Lloyd Mangrum, no mean putter himself. "Every time he putted I was sure the ball would stop just short of the hole. But it never did. The ball always seemed to have one more turn left in it. It would creep up to the hole—to the right side of the hole yet!—look in, and then roll over the lip. This happened whether he was three feet from the cup or 30."

Locke used a wooden-shafted blade putter then that he has been using all his life. It is several inches longer than standard, and Locke grips it at the extreme end. He advises against changing the position of the grip for different lengths of putts, and he employs the reverse overlapping grip. He uses a closed stance with his weight evenly balanced, the ball played opposite the left foot.

He addresses the ball on the toe of the putter. Copying from Hagen, he hoods the face on the backstroke and pulls it slightly inside. He then returns the blade in such a way that it strikes the ball in the center of the blade and not the toe, where he addresses it. All the while, he attempts to keep his left arm and the shaft, from the elbow to the clubhead, in one piece, restricting the motion to the arms rather than the wrists. Although he advocates that you stroke with a follow-through that is the same length as the backstroke, in practice he gives the impression of almost half-jabbing the ball.

At any rate, it goes inexorably into the hole.

AVOIDING THREE-PUTT GREENS

By Cary Middlecoff

Memphis, Tennessee

I maintain that you should try to make every putt you step up to, regardless of the putt's length. You are never likely to make a putt simply by trying to lag the ball into the vicinity of the hole. As a result of such boldness, I must admit you may frequently leave yourself some fairly long putts coming back. Under such circumstances, the tendency of most golfers is to be timid on the return putt. In nearly every instance, however, boldness will pay off. Your line, of course, is your chief concern, since on a short putt distance is an almost negligible factor. *Actually, the line has been indicated for you by your first putt. Naturally, it will follow about the same line coming back. All you have to do, then, is line up your putt along this line and stroke it with confidence.* Keep in mind that the grain will be just the opposite on your second putt from what it was on your first. If, therefore, you putted with the grain on your first putt, be sure to putt the ball very firmly on the return putt.

PUTTING UNDER PRESSURE

By Jack Fleck

Tarzana, California

Of course, putting under pressure is largely a matter of nerve. But there are physical and mental characteristics that can help ease the strain.

First of all, I like to keep myself well balanced when addressing a putt. This remedies the common fault of placing too much weight on one set of muscles, say, those of the left leg. Also, I like to take my stance with both feet square to the line, not with the left withdrawn. And I think it is more natural, and hence more comfortable, not to make the stance too wide.

The ball is stroked with a combination of the arms and the wrists. My shoulders never enter into the stroke unless my putts are very long, when I am, in effect, approach putting. On shorter putts of about five or six feet, I find it is best not to play for any break outside the edge of the hole, unless, of course, the break is obviously much greater. Instead, I try to play a slight break inside the hole by hitting the ball firmly.

As I stand over the ball, I make a conscious effort to block out all distractions such as the grain of the green, bite marks and footprints. I try to think positively. And that positive thought is always the same: Get the ball in the cup! *While thinking this, I keep my eyes glued directly over the ball, and I keep them there until well after the putt has actually been struck.*

CURING THE YIPS

By John McMullin

Fair Oaks, California

Many of the leading players in golf employ a forward press before taking their putters back. Some even do this unconsciously. There's a very good reason for this. To me, the forward press is a priceless tension breaker. I don't think it's possible to putt well if the putter is taken back from a dead stop. It's more likely you'll jerk the blade a bit off line if you start the putting backstroke without a forward press. My advice to anyone not using the forward press while putting is to *start with the hands directly over the ball, then press them forward about three or four inches, keeping the head and the rest of the body motionless. Start the putting backstroke from the most advanced point of the forward press. Don't move the hands back to the point where you started and then take the blade back. This puts an extra and unneeded motion into the stroke. Make sure that as your hands press forward, you don't open the blade of the putter. The blade should remain square to the ball and perhaps a little hooded.* Once you've developed the habit of using the forward press while putting, it'll become second nature and you won't even think about it. I find that the forward press helps me eliminate yips, promotes a sounder, smoother, steadier stroke. I'm a "stiff-wristed" putter and find that in my case the forward press serves to cock my wrists for the putt. I merely press forward and take the putter blade back at the completion for the press. There's virtually no wrist movement from then on, on my shorter putts. To me, the most beneficial aspect of the forward press is that it relaxes me to the point where I can hit the putt in less than perfect fashion and still get a very good result.

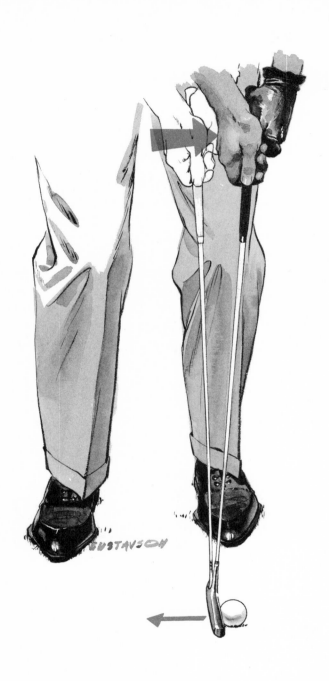

USING A HEAVY PUTTER

By Bob Goetz

Tulsa, Oklahoma

In my two-and-a-half years on tour I have noticed that many of the better putters use heavy putters. Experimentation and experience have taught me that using a heavy putter—say, one weighing about 17 ounces—promotes a more consistent and more predictable stroke. I believe it is true that it is easier to control a heavier putter, too. Imagine swinging a shaft without a clubhead, and you can readily appreciate what a difference clubhead weight makes in the consistency and control of the stroke. A golfer's hands change imperceptibly from day to day, Jug McSpaden used to say, and Jug used to use a 27-ounce putter to offset changes in his hands. Now, I'm not advocating that anyone use a 27-ounce putter, but McSpaden serves to support my contention that a heavier putter stabilizes the stroke; it's better because the putter head does most of the work. It is important to have a putter that has clubhead "feel." And here's another thing to consider when you buy a putter: Always make sure where dead center on the putter face is. The little line in the center of many putters does not necessarily mark the center or ideal hitting point; usually it serves to indicate a point equidistant between the ends of the putter head. *You can determine dead center by bouncing a ball along the putter face until you get to a place where there is no torque or "give."* Mark this spot. It is the spot best suited to contact the ball for greater consistency.

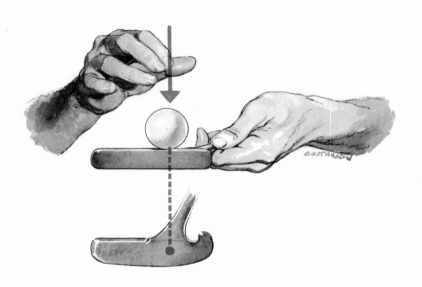

WOMEN'S DEADLIEST WEAPON

By Louise Suggs

My victory in the Palm Beach par-three invitation golf tournament last year convinced me that good putting can be a woman golfer's deadliest weapon.

I defeated 12 men pros as well as the women in that contest, primarily because my putting was exceptionally sharp. As far as I know, a woman has never before won a mixed tournament. But there's no reason why it shouldn't happen again and again, now that it's been proved that such a feat is possible. I've contended for a long time that, despite their decided disadvantage on the long game, women can beat men with their short games.

In the Palm Beach tournament, the odds were more balanced than they would ordinarily be because we were playing a short course. Every hole was a par-three, which means that the real test of skill rested on the short game. And on that occasion the hard work I had done to develop and refine my short game was justified.

It's my hope that what happened in Palm Beach will inspire women to put real thought and effort into their short games—particularly their putting.

Women on the whole are pretty decent putters. But there's no reason why they shouldn't be superb putters. This is one skill that doesn't involve strength, which means that a woman should be at least as good at it as any man. Putting is deceptive, however. It seems far easier than it is. And that's just why so many women neglect putting practice. They feel that they ought to spend their time practicing more challenging aspects of the game.

But they're wrong. Nothing could be more challenging than putting, or more important to your final score. In fact, it's the player who is putting well throughout a tournament who usually wins.

Even when women are well aware of all the complicated factors involved in putting, they don't necessarily practice more often. Frequently, they simply don't have the time. But I suspect that there's another reason: Temperamentally, women are more impulsive than men. They dislike having to analyze, deliberate, weigh and measure each shot. Men, on the other hand, love it. It's part of their nature. To women this sort of thing is unnatural. They don't train themselves to think that way. But there's no reason why they can't.

If your putting has been poor, or if you want to become an even better putter than you now are, try to get into the habit of practicing a few minutes each day and analyze what you're doing. Don't just haphazardly hit putts. If you don't know much about greens, learn to study them. Find out what makes a green slower or faster; how the grain will affect your ball; what happens on a sidehill lie; when you hit into the wind or when it rains. Find the individual putting stance, grip and swing that are best for you.

Consistent practice and analysis should produce good results in both your putting and your score within a reasonably short time.

12. PRACTICE PUTTING AND CHIPPING INDOORS THIS WINTER

By Jackson Bradley, PGA

River Oaks Country Club

Houston, Texas

Ben Hogan once said: "Golfers who don't live in Southern California are victims of circumstance." He was referring to the long, enforced winter layoff, which can be damaging to even a good regular golfer and downright disastrous for the spasmodic or once-a-week player. Golfers who have to go into a kind of physical hibernation for almost six months each year can't possibly be as sharp as those who are fortunate enough to live in tropical climates. But, at the same time there is a lot that can be done to offset the ill effects of the long winter layoff.

One unfortunate aspect of living in a cold climate is the general bodily debilitation that sets in during the winter. People who would ordinarily continue a program of regular outdoor exercise simply stop with the first snowflake. Overheated apartments, offices and houses; the restrictions of heavy clothing; tense body-bracing in the face of icy blasts; the tendency to party more and drink more (to forget the weather) and the unavoidable just-sitting-around—all these play a part in tearing down a physical well-being that barely has a chance to get built up during the summer.

But if you must hibernate for approximately six months a year, the first thing I advocate is a regular—I repeat: *regular*—program of physical exercise. Now, I don't mean 50 push-ups daily. You know how much of an athlete you are. But, I *do* say: keep in shape. No one can put his muscles in storage for six months and take them out good as new in the spring.

Make this an automatic habit. Get up in the morning. Go to the largest space in the room and *stretch*. Really try to grab hold of the ceiling. Then relax. Do this three or four times. Now take some good, deep breaths of air—really fill up that chest—then blow it out. Next swing your arms and body in a big, free arc. Rotate those hips and swing those arms. Try to imagine that you are throwing water out of large pans as far as it will go. By this time you should start to feel pretty loose. I'll guarantee you'll feel awake. Now if you want to throw in a few deep knee bends, you'll be helping to keep those all-important legs in shape. Do this every day for ten or 15 minutes. It's the regularity that's the main thing. And I promise you'll hit that course like a tiger when spring comes around.

So much for general body maintenance. Now for things you can do at home to keep your golf game in shape. In fact, not only keep what you have, but improve on it.

Now if you can, set up a practice target in the basement or garage for your long game (and this I heartily recommend). You must, however, concentrate on your short game with indoor practice during the winter months.

One of the most destructive manifestations of a long layoff from golf is the loss of "feel," or "touch," in your hands. Regular practice—once again, it's the regularity that's important—on your home-made pitch-and-putt course will keep you from feeling as if your hands belonged to somebody else when you step out on the course in the spring. The only materials you need are an ordinary water tumbler, a roll of adhesive tape, a cardboard carton approximately two feet wide by two feet high, and an old piece of carpet or a fiber door mat that simulates grass. Cut a window in the center of one side of the carton approximately 12 inches by 10 inches. Now find a nice, quiet spot in the house, with carpeting or a rug on the floor, and place the carton against a wall so that it will stay firm. You can place some heavy objects inside for added anchorage. Then put a thin book under the front edge in order to tilt the carton slightly upward. Be sure there is enough room in front of the carton so you can practice shots preferably up to ten feet away. Don't forget to put your mat down so you don't gouge holes in the floor. Now the chipping area of your course is ready. For putting practice, take your water tumbler and lay it on its side on the floor. Then take two 12 inch strips of adhesive tape and put one on the floor pointing in a direct line toward the mouth of the glass. A good practice distance from the cup is three to six feet.

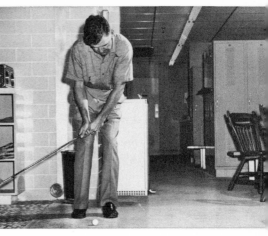

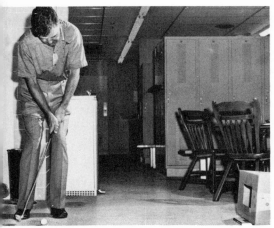
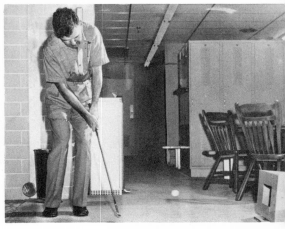

You will note in the illustration that I have placed the second 12-inch strip of adhesive on a line slightly inside of the first tape to form a narrow "Y". These strips of tape make valuable guide lines for putting practice. Make certain that you have *good lighting* in your practice area. With that, your pitch-and-putt course is complete.

The importance of this type of practice is two-fold. It keeps your grip and touch in shape and gives you a chance to develop a fine chipping and putting system. I believe and teach that chipping and putting are closely related. In both shots, the main objective is to create a *forward-rolling,* ground-hugging motion of the ball, with as little side-spin as possible. The most important thing to observe is this: There is very little change in the position of the clubhead in relation to the line of flight throughout the swing. In other words, the swing is similar to the action of a pendulum, rather than the arc-like motion of an opening and closing door. Now you are thinking: If this is so, why the second piece of tape inside the line of flight for putting and chipping? For this reason: The club should be drawn back slightly inside the line of flight in the backswing of both shots, but the clubface should *not open* on the backswing or *close* on the follow-through. This is most important. Your wrists control this action, so hold them steady and, as I said, swing the club as if it were a pendulum, keeping the blade square to the hole. The back view of the chip shot really illustrates what I mean. With the pendulum principle firmly established in your mind, the perfection of the chip shot depends on a natural, unhurried swing away from the ball and then the *feel* of the clubhead releasing its force through the ball. Note that the position of the clubface at the finish of the swing is similar to the address position. I'm using a six-iron, a club I use a great deal on chip shots with good results.

In the putting illustrations, I've employed exactly the same pendulum stroke—there is no opening of the clubface in the backswing. It feels as if the left wrist works under and inside the line, then straight out to the target on the line of the putt. I believe in a simple stance with my right foot dropped back a couple of inches. This procedure enables me to visualize the natural pattern the putter should follow. The force line, once again, is slightly inside to straight-through.

So, let's get with it. Like your general physical exercise, it is the establishment of a *regular* practice system that is most important. Don't go at it hot and heavy for a couple of hours at a time and then forget about

196

it for several weeks. Ten minutes' practice a day will produce much more impressive results than two hours once a month.

If you follow the suggestions I've outlined above, I'm not promising they'll call you "One-putt," or "Tarzan," but I do promise this: You'll know what you're doing around the greens when you start to play in the spring, and your body will be in shape to get the most out of your long game.

GOLF EXTRA: THE CHAMP'S CLINIC

By Jimmy Demaret

PROBLEM: I haven't been playing very long—only a year and a half. I hear all the golfers talking all the time about their wedge. Do you think I should buy one? Would it really help take strokes off my game? Right now I use a nine-iron in place of the wedge, but I'll get one if you think I should.—Virginia Kirkland, Los Angeles, Calif.

ANSWER: Chances are, Virginia, that you are not quite ready for a wedge. It's an all but worthless club unless you learn how to use it properly. The technique differs somewhat from the technique of the nine-iron, because the wedge has a flange on the sole which raises the front edge slightly off the turf, thus permitting you to add extra bite to the ball. Unless, however, you know how to take advantage of this flange, there isn't much point in using the club in place of your nine-iron. Stick to the niblick for the time being. After you have thoroughly learned the technique of it, then consult your local professional about buying a wedge.

PROBLEM: I am seventeen, and have been playing golf for five months. I am shooting in the low forties for nine holes and have a full set of clubs except a wedge. Which type should I buy, sand, pitching or all-purpose wedge?—Don Braaten, Forest Grove, Ore.

ANSWER: If you don't have a sand wedge, you had getter get one. You can pitch with it, but you can't possibly play a sand shot correctly with a pitching wedge.

PROBLEM: I know it is next to impossible for you to explain a certain flaw in a person's swing without seeing him execute it, but there is a question I have that this problem will not enter into. I have read many books and articles regarding confidence while putting. None has given me the right mental attitude toward it. My pro tells me that mechanically I'm fine. Could you please explain how to go about getting confidence on the putting green?—Willie Nevin, Piedmont, Calif.

ANSWER: Try making your target larger. By this I mean, don't try to hole all your putts. Rather, try to get the ball within two feet of the hole if you are 20 feet away, three feet if you are 30 feet, four feet if you are 40 feet, and so on.

PROBLEM: I have a terrible problem in my pitch-and-run shots from the apron to the green. I mainly use an eight-iron on these shots. Whenever the shot calls for a nine-iron, however, I choke and hit the ball about halfway to the pin. Do you think I should stay with the eight-iron, or what?—Rand Lazaroff, Roosevelt, N.Y.

ANSWER: These shots are much easier to play with a more straight-faced club—a four- or five-iron. Play the shot with the feet close together, right elbow close into the side, and the club choked.

PROBLEM: On a long putt I generally slide to the right of the hole. It looks as if I am lined-up okay. But if I leave the putter head in its original position and sight to the pole from behind the putter, the head is definitely aimed to the right—just where the ball goes. Is this just a matter of practice or am I missing some basic?—J. R. Moss, O.D., Corydon, Ind.

ANSWER: This fault is a good deal more common than you might suspect. It has something to do—and as an optometrist you ought to know what—with being either "right-eyed" or "left-eyed," I don't know exactly which. As I understand the situation, one or the other does the primary sighting while the other focuses in on the image.

PROBLEM: I am 14 years old and have been playing golf for two years. I have a mallet-headed putter and would like to know what you consider a good putting stance. I stand with my feet about an inch apart and play the ball off the middle of my left foot.—Patrick Elliott, St. Louis, Mo.

ANSWER: The main essential in putting is to have your eyes directly over the back of the ball. The width of the stance is immaterial so long as you maintain good balance.

PROBLEM: Recently I have been able to pare several strokes off my game by punching my second shot into the green rather than trying to lift it in with an eight- or nine-iron. By playing short with a five- or six-iron and letting the ball kill its roll before hitting the green, I have been able to get on in regulation figures more consistently. Some of my friends criticize my methods. However, as some of the pros say, "It isn't how, it's how many." How do you feel about it?—Bob Tutt, San Francisco, Calif.

ANSWER: It is very risky to play a pitch-and-run from outside a radius of 30 yards. Also, you don't solve a problem by shying away from it. Why not take a lesson on pitch shots from your pro and equip yourself for all emergencies?

PROBLEM: I'm six and a half feet tall. I swing very upright and putt very upright. What type of putter do you recommend I use with my physique? —Wilbur "Stretch" Harris, Houston, Texas.

ANSWER: Putters are as much a matter of taste as neckties. Mallet-head, goose-neck, blade—it makes little difference what type you use, regardless of your physique. A really good putter can putt with a broom, if need be. I suggest you find one type you like and stick to it.

PROBLEM: I am 29, have played golf four-and-a-half years, and score around 78 to 82. After much practice I have learned to stop, draw and fade most of the irons from outside 40 or 50 yards. But one thing really bugs me. I know I could cut six or seven strokes off my game if I could get closer to the pin (especially to elevated greens) from within 40 or 50 yards. I can't seem to hit that delicate soft shot and consequently, on those long par threes, fours and fives, I leave myself very long putts or chip shots because of an inaccurate (distance-wise) second or third shot. How, and with what club does one execute this delicate approach?—Al Sym, Arlington, Va.

ANSWER: These delicate shots are best played with a nine-iron or pitching wedge, but the real fault may lie in your eyesight. Have you had a recent test?

PROBLEM: Today for the first time I broke 80 and was not satisfied. Maybe I am foolish, but I still figure there was room for improvement. I have the tendency to drop my left knee just before I take a chip shot that, on occasions, results in a shank or a poorly hit shot. What should I do, and is this the cause of my trouble?—James Balfe, Boston, Mass.

ANSWER: Play your chips with your hands and arms, no body move-ment.

PROBLEM: Just before I stroke my putt, I rest my putter on the ground behind the ball. I believe I read somewhere that the putter should barely touch the ground, that the full weight of the putter should not be on the ground. Is this correct?—Russ Kyle, St. Petersburg, Fla.

ANSWER: Barely touching the ground with the putter is a refinement de-veloped many years ago by the late Jerry Travers, one of the sharpest putters who ever lived. Unless you are a very good putter yourself, I sug-gest you leave such refinements to the experienced players.

PROBLEM: What is the longest distance an average weekend golfer should try to chip a ball? In practice, for example, I frequently dump out my shag balls and carry out the shag bag about 50 steps to serve as a tar-get. I then start my practice by pitching to the bag—beyond, to the right, left, etc. Now, by using a chipping stroke, I can easily chip the ball 40 to 50 yards. Does this kind of shot have a place in golf? Given a fairly good lie, which would you use—an all-carry pitch to the green or a chip that carries 40 yards and runs ten?—P. K. Connelly, West Lafayette, Ind.

ANSWER: It doesn't seem likely to me that you can chip—really chip—a ball 40 to 50 yards. What you are actually practicing is a pitch-and-run shot. As such, it definitely has a place in golf. It is, in fact, used frequently by the British, and can be an invaluable shot to an unbanked green, par-ticularly when the wind is blowing.

PROBLEM: I have been bothered by "choking up" on short and long putts in matches. On the practice green, I'm pretty good. Are there any special tricks to keep a golfer relaxed while putting?—Joseph Ormond, M.D., Norwalk, Conn.

ANSWER: Try using a forward press before stroking the putt. It removes a great deal of tension. If you think it's the concentration factor that is bothering you, keep your mind on one certain aspect of the stroke itself and forget about the match or your score.

PROBLEM: *I've lost my putting touch! All my putts go to the left of the hole and stop two or three feet short. Can you please help me?—Charles Gillordi, Plainfield, Conn.*

ANSWER: Keep that clubface at right angles to the direction line after you have stroked the ball. This will usually prevent a pulled putt.

PROBLEM: *My big problem is getting loft on a ball over a sand trap or a small hill onto the green with a maximum of backspin. This shot is particularly difficult for me when the ball lies directly behind the obstacle and the pin is just opposite it.—Roger Maurice, Detroit, Mich.*

ANSWER: Keep your hands ahead of the clubhead at the address. Use your wrists to hit the ball firmly. Don't try to scoop it. The club will provide the necessary loft and bite if the shot is hit crisply. Most important, forget the hazard exists when you're thinking about the shot. It'll help develop confidence.

PROBLEM: *A companion and myself have had an argument that we haven't been able to resolve. He says that when exploding a ball from soft sand in a bunker, the clubface comes into actual contact with the ball even though the properly executed shot hits the sand as much as three inches behind the ball. I say that it is the force of the sand exploding in front of the clubface that lifts the ball from the sand, especially on short shots. Who is right?—Ivor D. Foster, Hinton, Alberta, Canada.*

ANSWER: You are.

PROBLEM: *Is there any fundamental difference—or should there be—in the way you stroke an approach putt and a short putt? Do you think putts of all distances should be hit with the same kind of stroke?—D. R. Troyer, St. Louis, Mo.*

ANSWER: Definitely keep to one method of putting, and the best putters are those who stroke the ball smoothly. There are three basic rules to good putting: a square stance; eye directly over back of ball; head static throughout the stroke.

PROBLEM: Can you inform me how to go about judging distance with my chip shots? Every time I chip I end up knocking the ball ten feet past the cup or end up leaving it ten feet short. As a result of making so many horrible misses, I have lost all faith in my ability to chip. By the way, I always use a nine-iron.—Carl Swanson, Minneapolis, Minn.

ANSWER: The first thing you ought to do is leave your nine-iron in your bag. You can't chip with a niblick. You pitch with it. By trying to chip with it you are unnecessarily lofting the ball, with the result that the shot has little or no control. Try using your five-iron, instead. Then, when addressing the ball, visualize the ball rolling to the hole much as it might roll if you had tossed it with your hand. As a matter of fact, you might try just that—tossing the ball to the cup underhanded. Once you have the feel of the distance with your hand, it won't be much of a problem transferring this feeling to the technique of the chip. And once you have the *feel* of the chip, you should have no trouble judging the proper length.

Set in Times Roman
Format by Stanley M. Wheatman
Manufactured by The Haddon Craftsmen, Inc.
Published by Harper & Brothers, New York